Instant Art for Lent and Easter

Compiled and illustrated
by
Kathryn Atkins

First published in 1995 in Great Britain by
KEVIN MAYHEW LTD
Rattlesden
Bury St Edmunds, Suffolk IP30 0SZ

Catalogue No 1396040
ISBN 0 86209 746 0

Cover by Sara Silcock
Typesetting by Louise Hill
Printed in Great Britain

Introduction

Bring the Easter story alive with this wide variety of Lent and Easter activities, including an Easter 3-D scene, frieze, mobile, cards, puzzles, exciting action models, and a special series of worksheets for Lent. This collection has something for a wide variety of ages, and is ideal for use in many situations: day schools, mid-week clubs, family services, Sunday schools, nurseries, playgroups or at home.

• copyright

Material in this book is copyright-free, provided that it is used for the purposes for which it is intended. (Reproduction of the contents of this book for commercial purposes is subject of the usual copyright restrictions.)

• suggestions for use

For some of the activities you may want to tell the story in some way, e.g. drama, storytelling, puppets, overhead projector drawing. Other activities could be used for more extended craft sessions through Lent and Easter week. The series of six paired activity sheets and craft sheets for Lent, called Lent Lights, could be used as a weekly (or twice weekly) session leading up to Easter. Alternatively, they could be used as a series at any time of the year, if you blank out 'Lent Lights' before you photocopy the sheets.

You will need to photocopy one for each child – unless you are working together on a group project, for example, assembling the Easter model. Most of the activities need to be photocopied onto card, but some only need paper. Always encourage the children to colour in parts of any model *before* assembling it.

• photocopying onto card

Most photocopiers will take a fine grade of card, and photocopying models straight onto card rather than gluing a paper copy to card achieves a much better and quicker result.

Fine card (A4 size) suitable for photocopying should be available in large packs from suppliers of photocopy paper or from printers. The card will probably need to be *hand fed* into the photocopier, but this does not take too long.

• equipment required

It is a good idea to make up one model yourself at home at first – this gives you a knowledge of the steps to follow and the equipment you will need, and gives the children a visual demonstration of the finished model.

Good Scissors – an essential, but should have round points.

Colouring Pens – cheap packs of felt tip pens are readily available.

Crayons – better for young children for some of the activities.

Glue – solid stick glue with a twist-up end is best. It is quite expensive, but holds in place well for small tabs etc and is not too messy.

Paper Fasteners – available from stationers in boxes of 100 (size 15mm is a useful size).

Sharp point – a compass is useful to pierce holes before inserting paper fasteners. *NB PIERCING HOLES ONLY TO BE DONE BY AN ADULT FOR SAFETY.*

Craft knife – only to be used by an *ADULT FOR SAFETY*. This is useful in some models for cutting slits or small windows. This should be done before the children's craft session. Just make the appropriate slits/cuts in all the A4 sheets before pieces are cut out. Rest on a piece of hardboard.

Foldlines – are marked as follows and will be easier to fold if they are very lightly scored before folding.

– – – – – fold outwards (or 'mountain fold')

– · – · – · fold inwards (or 'valley fold')

• readers' responses

The Instant Art series has been developed in response to ideas and suggestions from those who have used earlier titles. We would welcome any comments you might wish to make on existing books, and ideas for new additions to the list are always carefully considered.

Contents

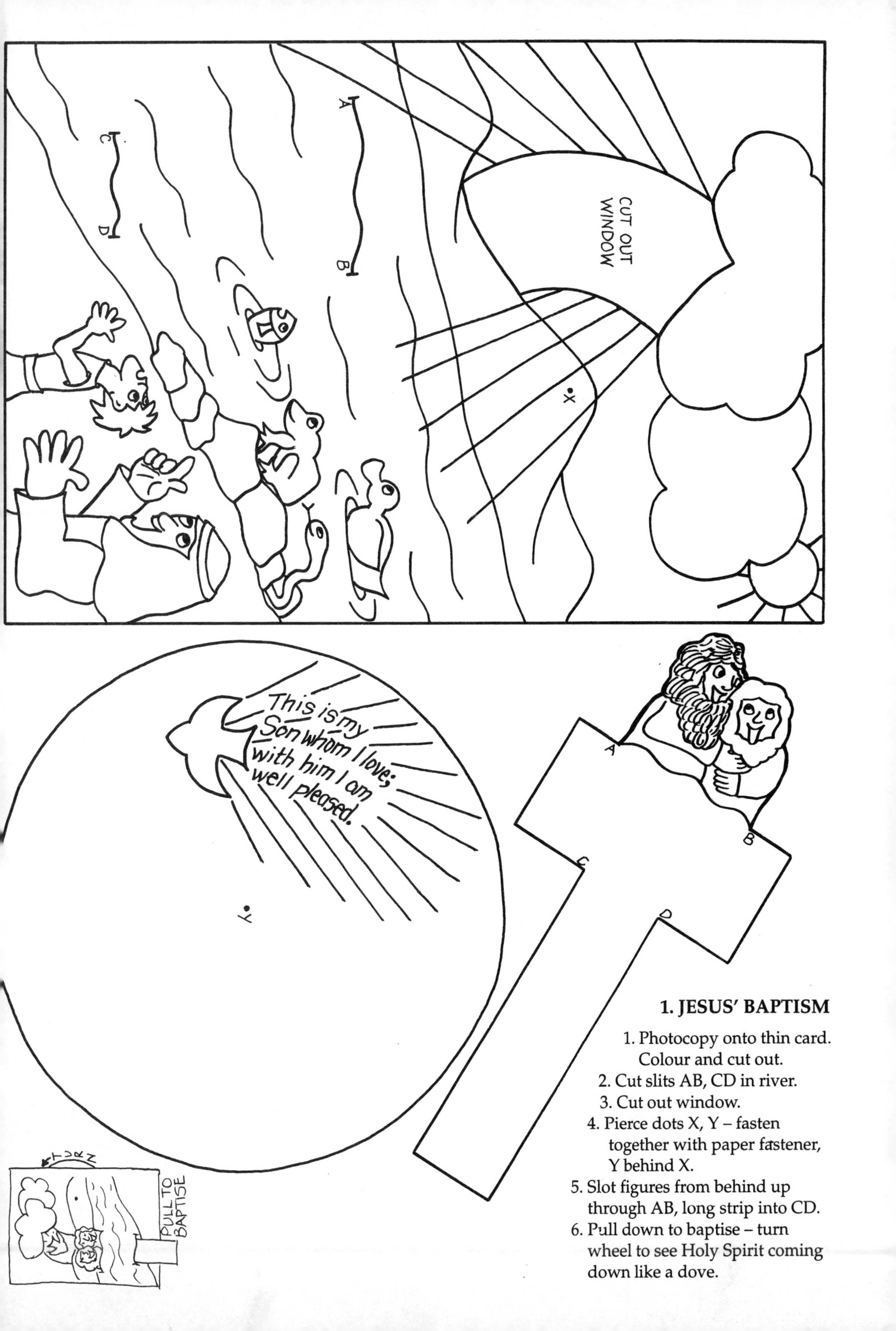

1. JESUS' BAPTISM

1. Photocopy onto thin card. Colour and cut out.
2. Cut slits AB, CD in river.
3. Cut out window.
4. Pierce dots X, Y – fasten together with paper fastener, Y behind X.
5. Slot figures from behind up through AB, long strip into CD.
6. Pull down to baptise – turn wheel to see Holy Spirit coming down like a dove.

2. TEMPTATIONS OF JESUS – SPINNER PART ONE

1. Photocopy onto thin card – this **and** following page.
2. Colour and cut out.
3. Cut out windows.
4. Pierce dots A and B.
5. Attach B behind A using paper fastener.
6. Turn to see temptations of Jesus.

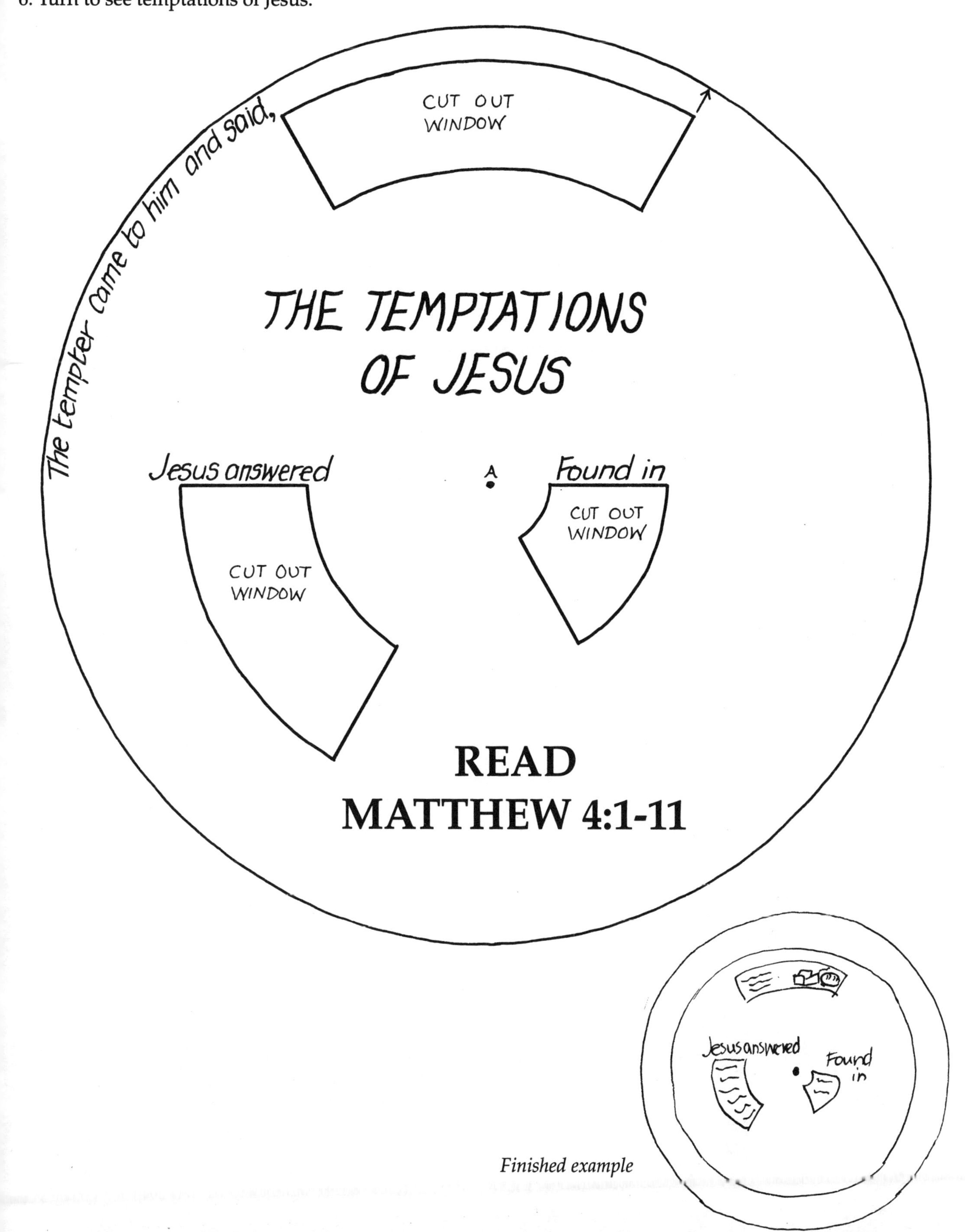

Finished example

3. TEMPTATIONS OF JESUS – SPINNER PART TWO

4. JESUS' TRANSFIGURATION – ACTION MODEL PART ONE

1. Photocopy this **and** following page onto thin card.
2. Colour and cut out.
3. Glue shiny paper or foil onto Jesus' shining clothes.
4. Fold tabs XY and VW on Jesus and glue to base folded at right angles.
5. Stick Moses and Elijah and Peter, James and John to model as shown.
6. Pierce dots A, B – attach B behind A using paper fastener.
7. For transfiguration, use shining clothes and fold out the cloud with God's voice.

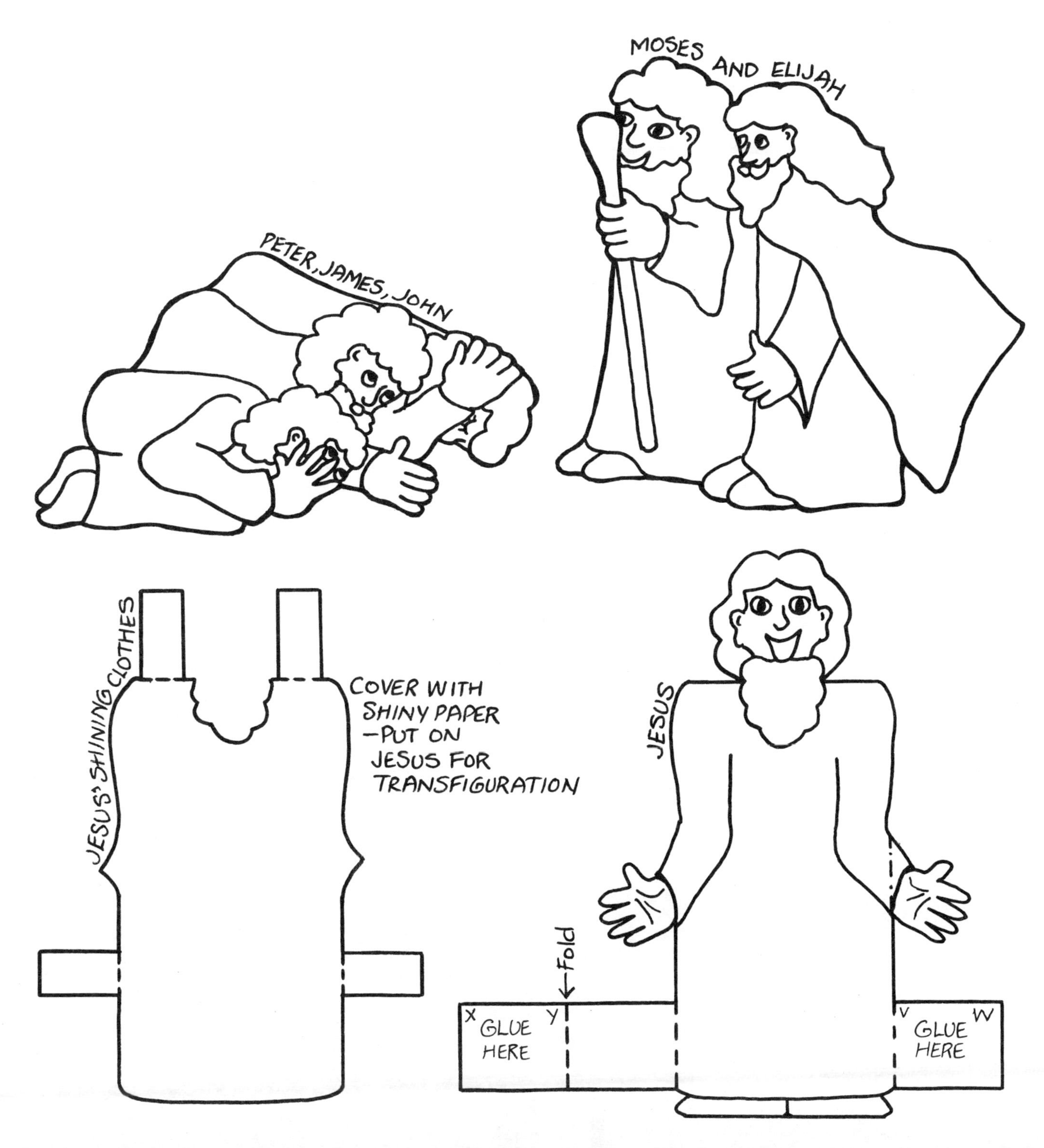

5. JESUS' TRANSFIGURATION – ACTION MODEL PART TWO

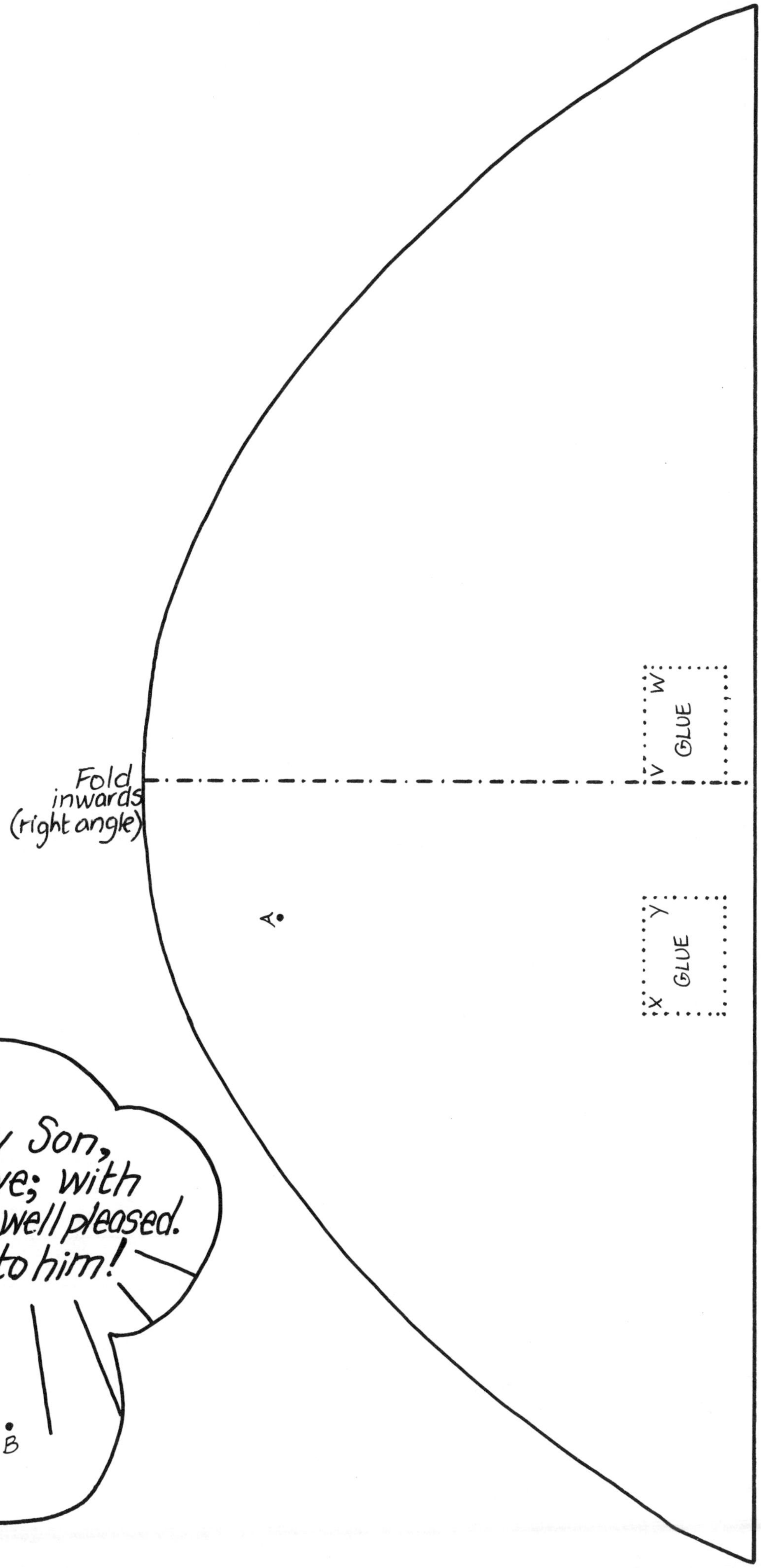

Fold
inwards
(right angle)

W

GLUE

V

A

Y

GLUE

X

This is my Son,
whom I love; with
him I am well pleased.
Listen to him!

B

6. MOTHER'S DAY GIFT BOX AND MINI HEART CARD

1. Photocopy onto thin card.
2. Colour and cut out.
3. Fold all foldlines – – – – outwards ('mountain')
   – . – . – inwards ('valley')
4. Glue hearts A and B to marked position on card – fold so that heart 'pops out'. Draw your own design on front.
5. Fold up box and glue tabs XY, VW in place.
6. fill box with sweets or pot-pourri. Slot slits together at top.

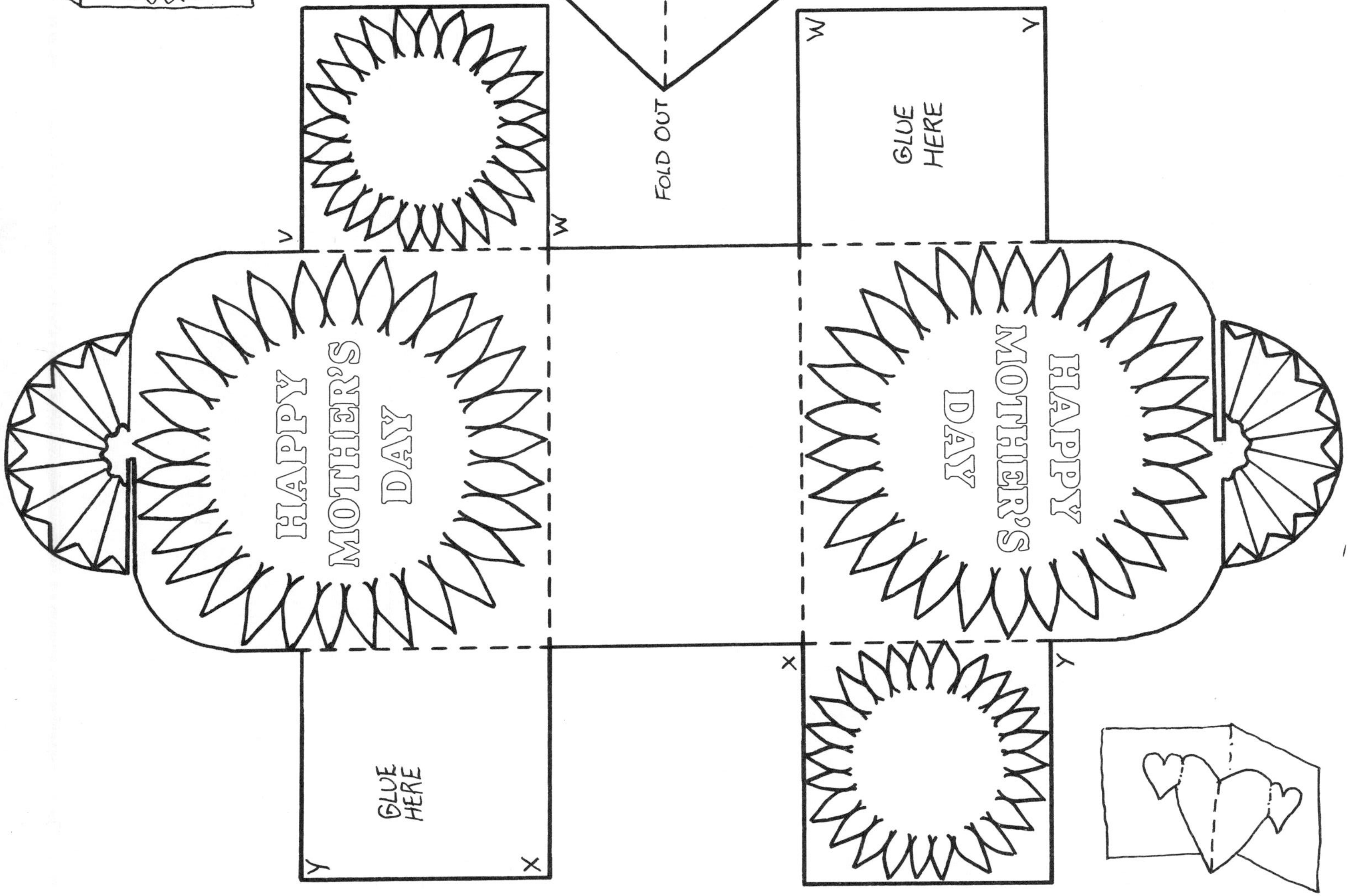

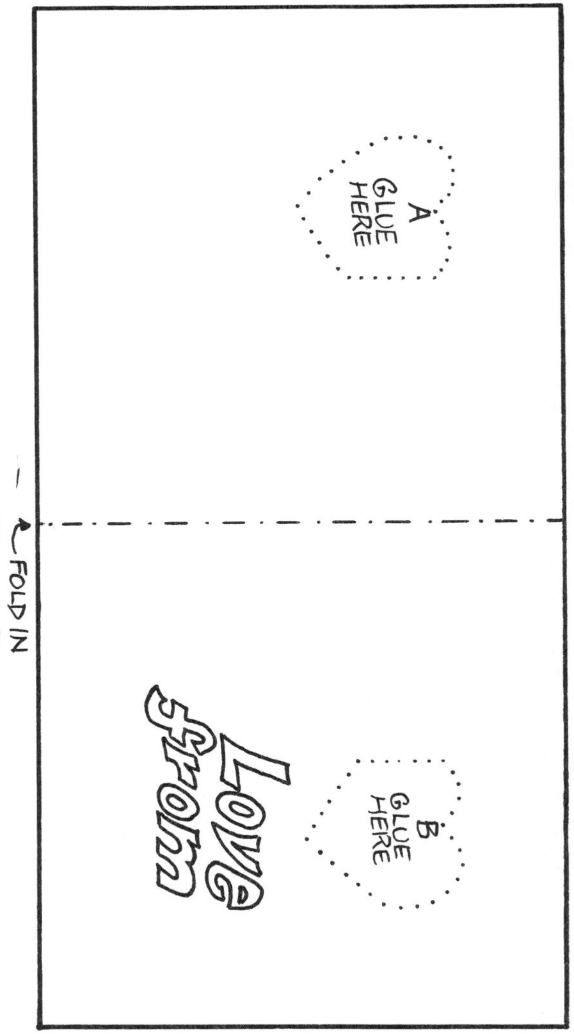

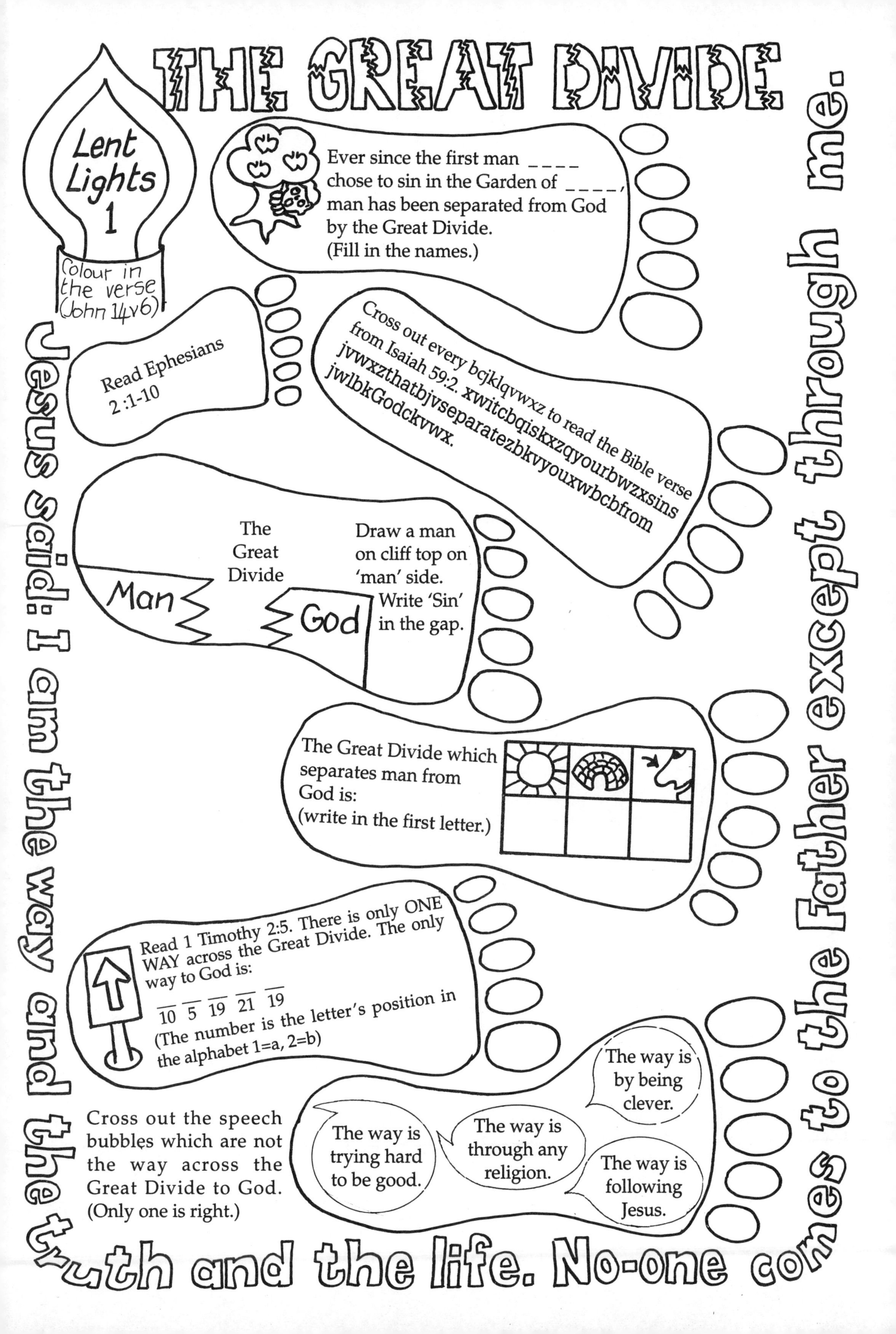

THE GREAT DIVIDE
Lent Lights 1
Colour in the verse (John 14v6)
Ever since the first man ____ chose to sin in the Garden of ____, man has been separated from God by the Great Divide. (Fill in the names.)
Read Ephesians 2:1-10
Cross out every bcjklqvwxz to read the Bible verse from Isaiah 59:2. xwitcbqiskxzqyourbwzxsins jvwxzthatbjvseparatezbkvyouxwbcbfrom jwlbkGodckvwx.
The Great Divide
Man
God
Draw a man on cliff top on 'man' side. Write 'Sin' in the gap.
The Great Divide which separates man from God is: (write in the first letter.)
Read 1 Timothy 2:5. There is only ONE WAY across the Great Divide. The only way to God is:
10 5 19 21 19
(The number is the letter's position in the alphabet 1=a, 2=b)
Cross out the speech bubbles which are not the way across the Great Divide to God. (Only one is right.)
The way is trying hard to be good.
The way is through any religion.
The way is by being clever.
The way is following Jesus.
Jesus said: I am the way and the truth and the life. No-one comes to the Father except through me.

8. LENT LIGHTS 1 – THE GREAT DIVIDE ACTION MODEL

1. Photocopy onto thin card and cut out.
2. Fold out on all foldlines.
3. Pierce dots A, B, C, D.
4. Glue all tabs and glue model together as an illustration.
5. Attach 'Jesus bridge' with paper fasteners – one through A then C, the other through B then D.
6. Glue man and crown onto top of Man and God sides of the Great Divide.
7. Lower 'Jesus bridge' to make a way to God across the Great Divide of Sin!

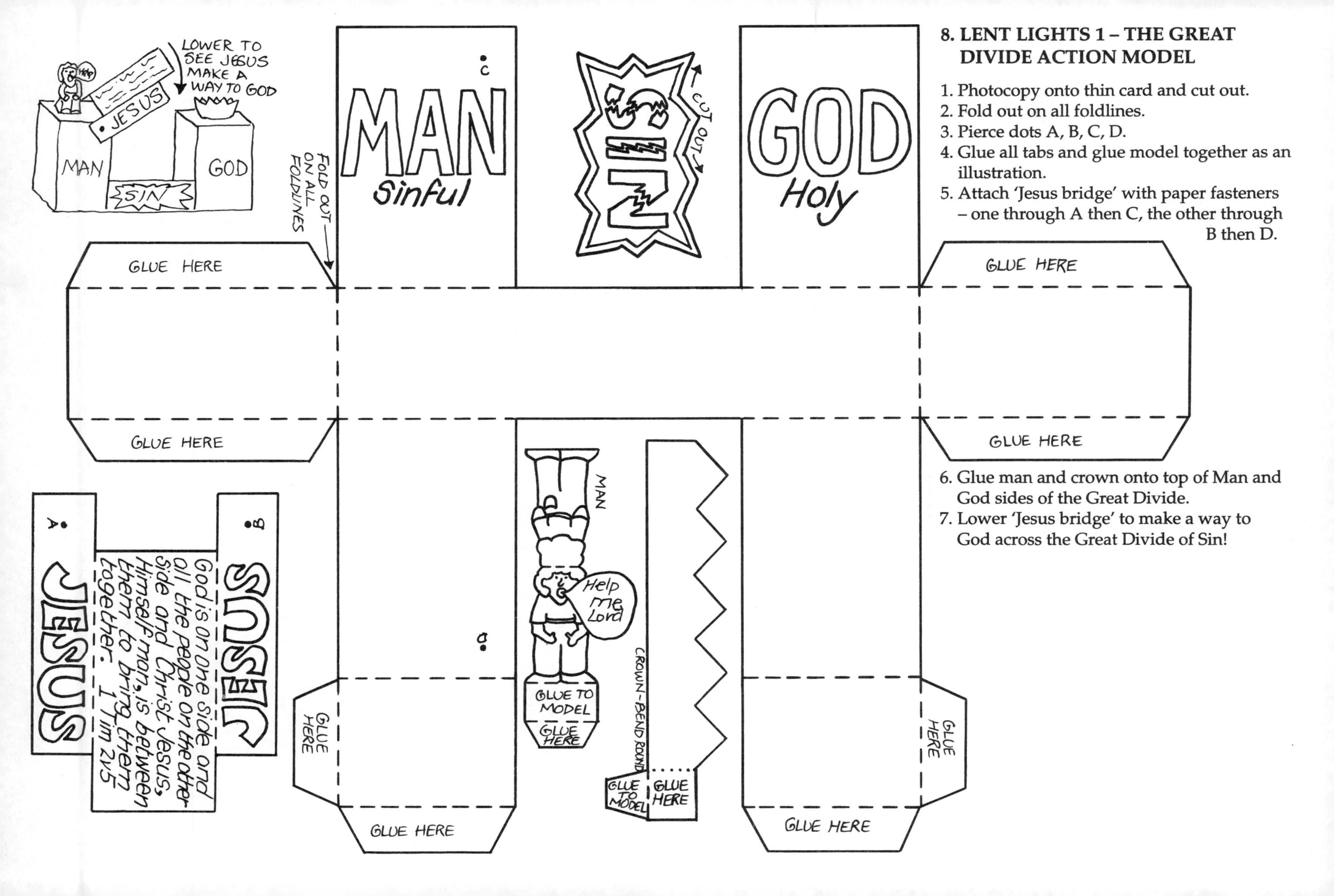

THE WINNER
Lent Lights 2
Colour in the verse (Col 2 v13-14)
THE WINNER
Jesus the King of Kings
Our list of sins was destroyed by
______ it to Christ's
______
(Fill in missing words)
Over 700 years before Jesus came God told Isaiah to write down prophecies which talked about Jesus and what he has won for us.
You can read some of this prophecy in Isaiah 53
Try Isaiah Chapter 53 verses 4-6
Q 1 W 2 E 3 R 4 T 5 Y 6 U 7 I 8 O 9 P 10
A 11 S 12 D 13 F 14 G 15 H 16 J 17 K 18 L 19 ; 20
Z 21 X 22 C 23 V 24 B 25 N 26 M 27 , 28 : 29 . 30
Use the keyboard to crack the code below about what Jesus has won for us by his sacrifice on the cross.
5 16 3 10 7 26 8 12 16 27 3 26 5 5 16 11 5
25 4 9 7 15 16 5 7 12 10 3 11 23 3 2 11 12 7 10 9 26
16 8 27 28 11 26 13 25 6 16 8 12 2 9 7 26 13 12
2 3 11 4 3 16 3 11 19 3 13 30
(Isaiah 53:5)
God forgave us all our sins; he cancelled the unfavourable record of our debts with its binding rules.... by nailing it to the cross.

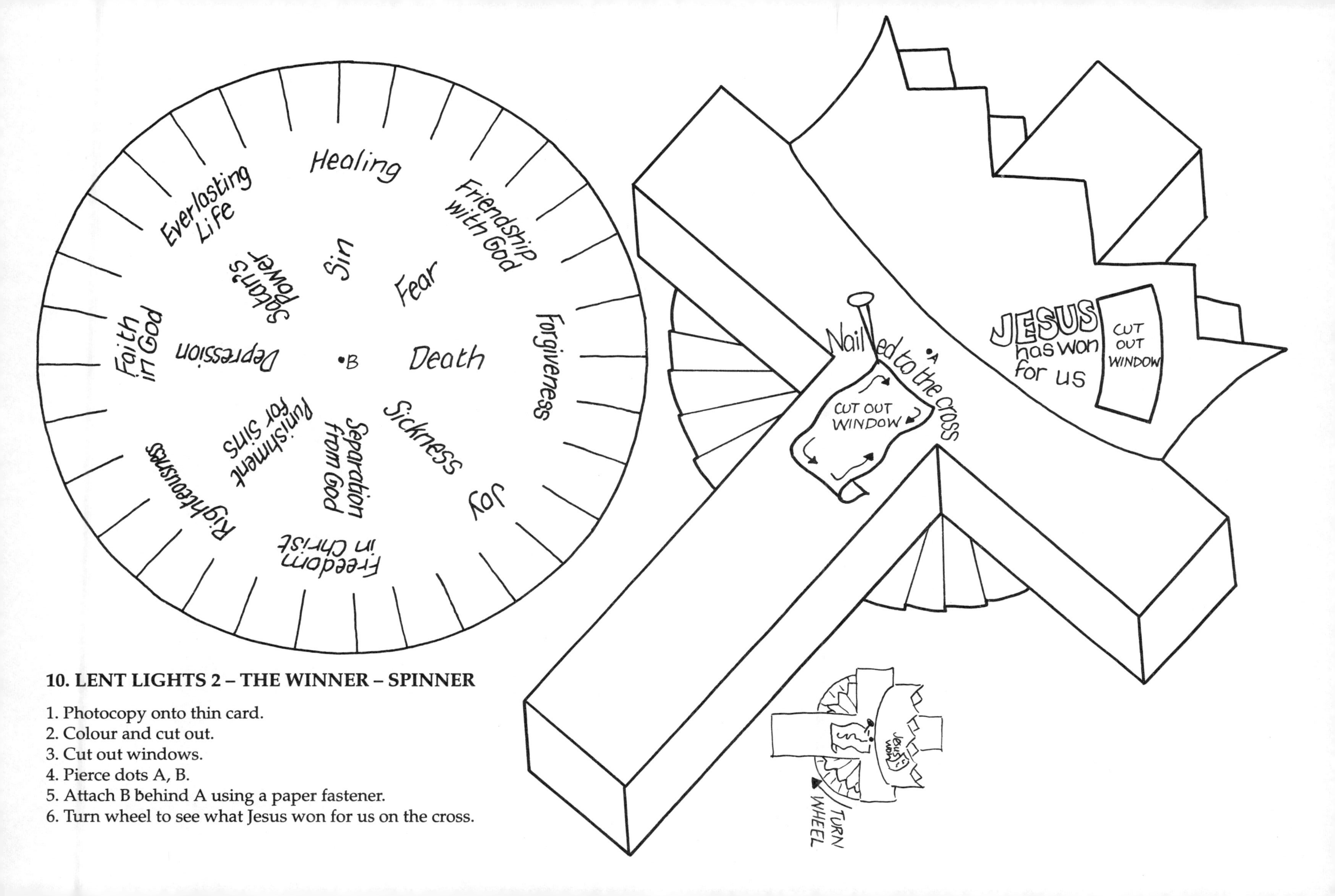

10. LENT LIGHTS 2 – THE WINNER – SPINNER

1. Photocopy onto thin card.
2. Colour and cut out.
3. Cut out windows.
4. Pierce dots A, B.
5. Attach B behind A using a paper fastener.
6. Turn wheel to see what Jesus won for us on the cross.

A NEW CREATION
Lent Lights 3
Colour in the verse (John 3v16)
Read the story of Nicodemus in John Chapter 3
Find the underlined words in the wordsearch puzzle.
O T H G I N M T S P
I S P I R I T E H K
W U R O R E T A W I
E M B A J K R C N N
J E S U S I U H I K
E D R O S N T E C W
W O L E L G H R A I
I C E T R D M T L B
S I N D N O C E S B
H N O L O M A N S A
T G I B A T E A U R
A Pharisee called Nicodemus came to see Jesus at night and said, 'Rabbi, we know you are a teacher who has come from 'God.'
Jesus told him, 'I tell you the truth – unless a man is born again he cannot see the kingdom of God.'
'How can a man be born when he is old?' Nicodemus asked. Jesus explained to the Jewish leader about being born into God's kingdom by water and the Holy Spirit.
ASK YOURSELF
Have I decided to follow Jesus?
Q. In what story does Nicodemus appear again?
A. Find out in John 19:38-42
The words in this message have all got turned round backwards – write them out the right way to make sense of it.
FI ENOYNA SI NI TSIRHC EH
SI A WEN NOITAERC; EHT DLO
SAH ENOG, EHT WEN SAH EMOC. (2 Cor 5:17)
For God so loved the world that he gave his one and only Son, that whoever believes in him shall not perish but have everlasting life.

12. LENT LIGHTS 3 –
A NEW CREATION
POP-UP ACTION MODEL
1. Photocopy onto thin card.
2. Colour girl/boy figure and draw in your face. Cut out oblong. Cut slits AB, CD.
3. Fold all foldlines - - - - outwards - · - · - · inwards.
4. Glue base of girl/boy BD to pop-out on card.
A
C
B
D
I am a new creation
B
D
I am a new creation
B
D

LIFE TO THE FULL
Lent Lights 4
Colour in the verse (John 10v10)
Read John 10v7-10
JESUS wants us to
(↑ Fill in the first letter of each object)
E
L
H
O
S
S
R
U
E
SATAN'S KINGDOM
J
S
GOD'S KINGDOM
D
E
S
X
B
N
S
A
You can only live life to the full in one of these two kingdoms. Draw your face in the right one.
Find the way from Satan's kingdom to God's kingdom. Collect the letters you find on the way to spell the only way to God's kingdom.
_ _ _ _ _.
This part of my life is private KEEP OUT
Draw a picture of yourself doing something you really enjoy. Let Jesus be part of everything you do – not just at church.
DON'T have any things in your life that you have to keep God out of.
Jesus said: I am the gate; whoever enters through me will be saved.... I have come that they may have life, and have it to the full.

14. LENT LIGHTS 4 – LIFE TO THE FULL MOBILE

1. Photocopy onto thin card.
2. Cut out and pierce all dots.
3. On the back of the four 'verse' pieces draw four pictures of things you enjoy doing.
4. Hang these from 'LIFE' piece using different length threads.

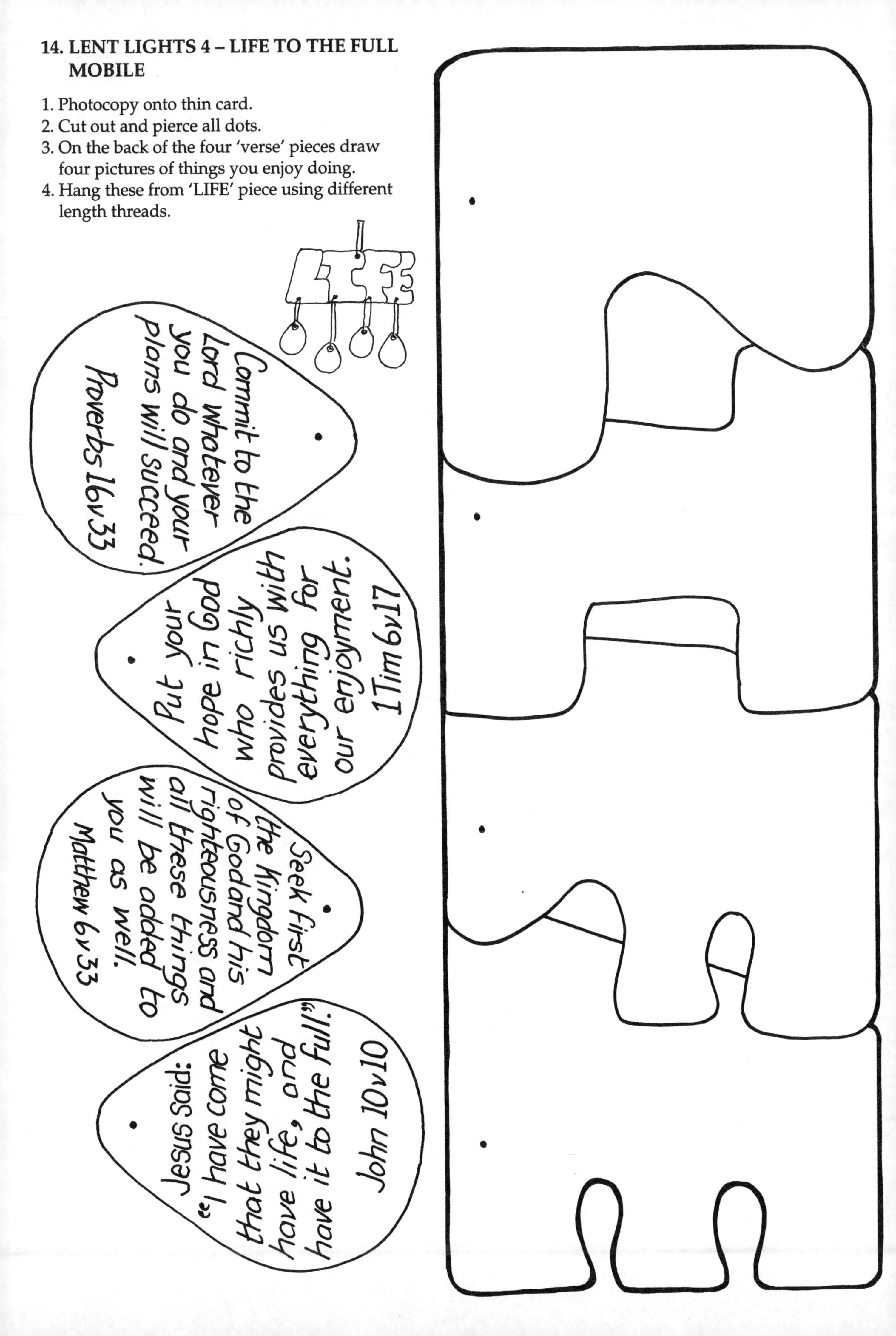

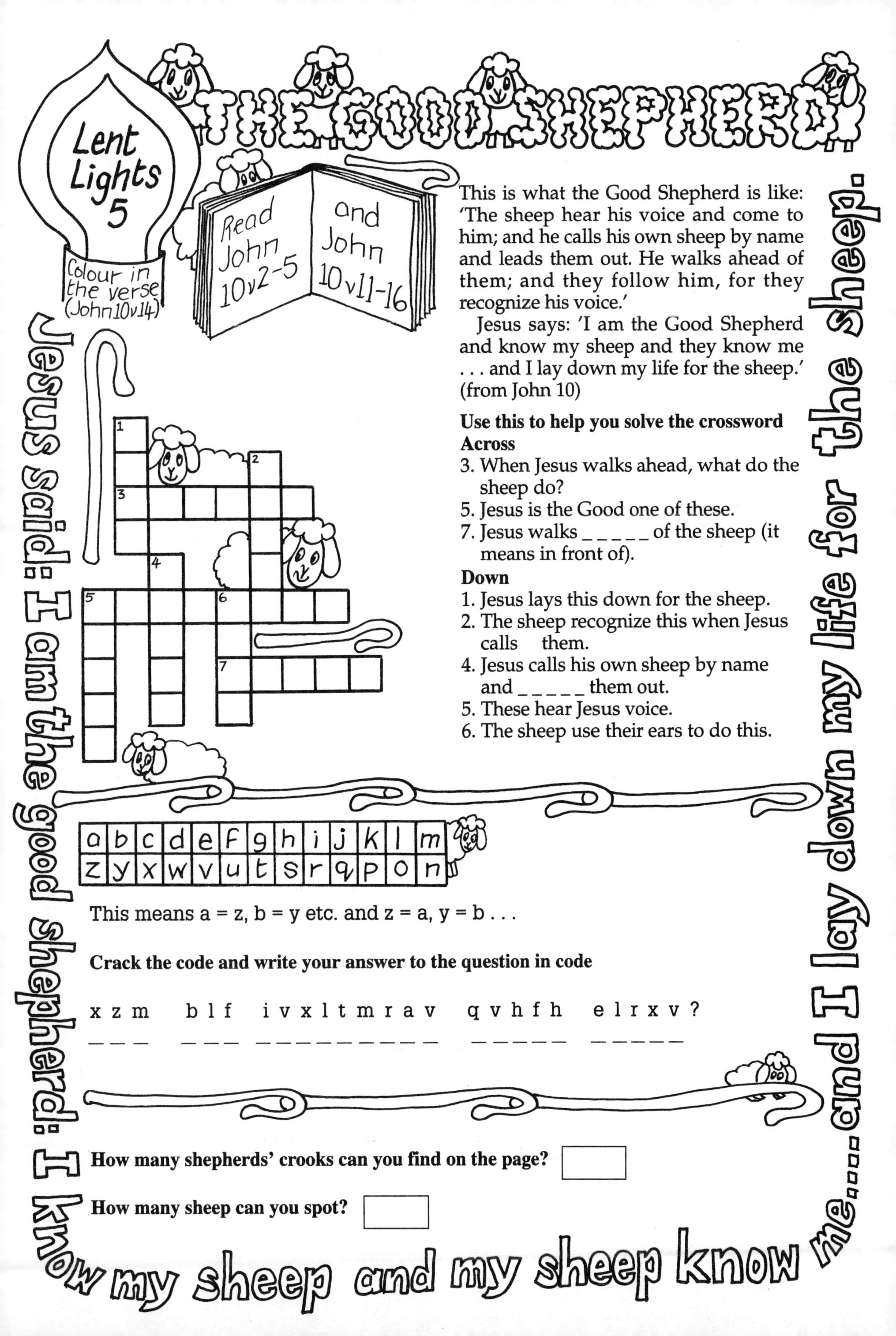

This is what the Good Shepherd is like: 'The sheep hear his voice and come to him; and he calls his own sheep by name and leads them out. He walks ahead of them; and they follow him, for they recognize his voice.'

Jesus says: 'I am the Good Shepherd and know my sheep and they know me . . . and I lay down my life for the sheep.' (from John 10)

Use this to help you solve the crossword

Across

3. When Jesus walks ahead, what do the sheep do?
5. Jesus is the Good one of these.
7. Jesus walks _ _ _ _ _ of the sheep (it means in front of).

Down

1. Jesus lays this down for the sheep.
2. The sheep recognize this when Jesus calls them.
4. Jesus calls his own sheep by name and _ _ _ _ _ them out.
5. These hear Jesus voice.
6. The sheep use their ears to do this.

This means a = z, b = y etc. and z = a, y = b . . .

Crack the code and write your answer to the question in code

x z m   b l f   i v x l t m r a v   q v h f h   e l r x v ?

_ _ _   _ _ _   _ _ _ _ _ _ _ _ _ _   _ _ _ _ _   _ _ _ _ _

How many shepherds' crooks can you find on the page? ☐

How many sheep can you spot? ☐

16. LENT LIGHTS 5 – THE GOOD SHEPHERD – OPEN DOOR CALENDAR.

1. Photocopy onto thin card.
2. Cut out, colour top piece.
3. NB **before** session with children, adult must cut the doors with craft knife round 3 sides on solid lines only – do not fold back at this stage.
4. Glue thin strip of back as marked, place front on top, line up edges carefully.
5. Open one door each day – it doesn't matter which day you start – follow instructions inside.

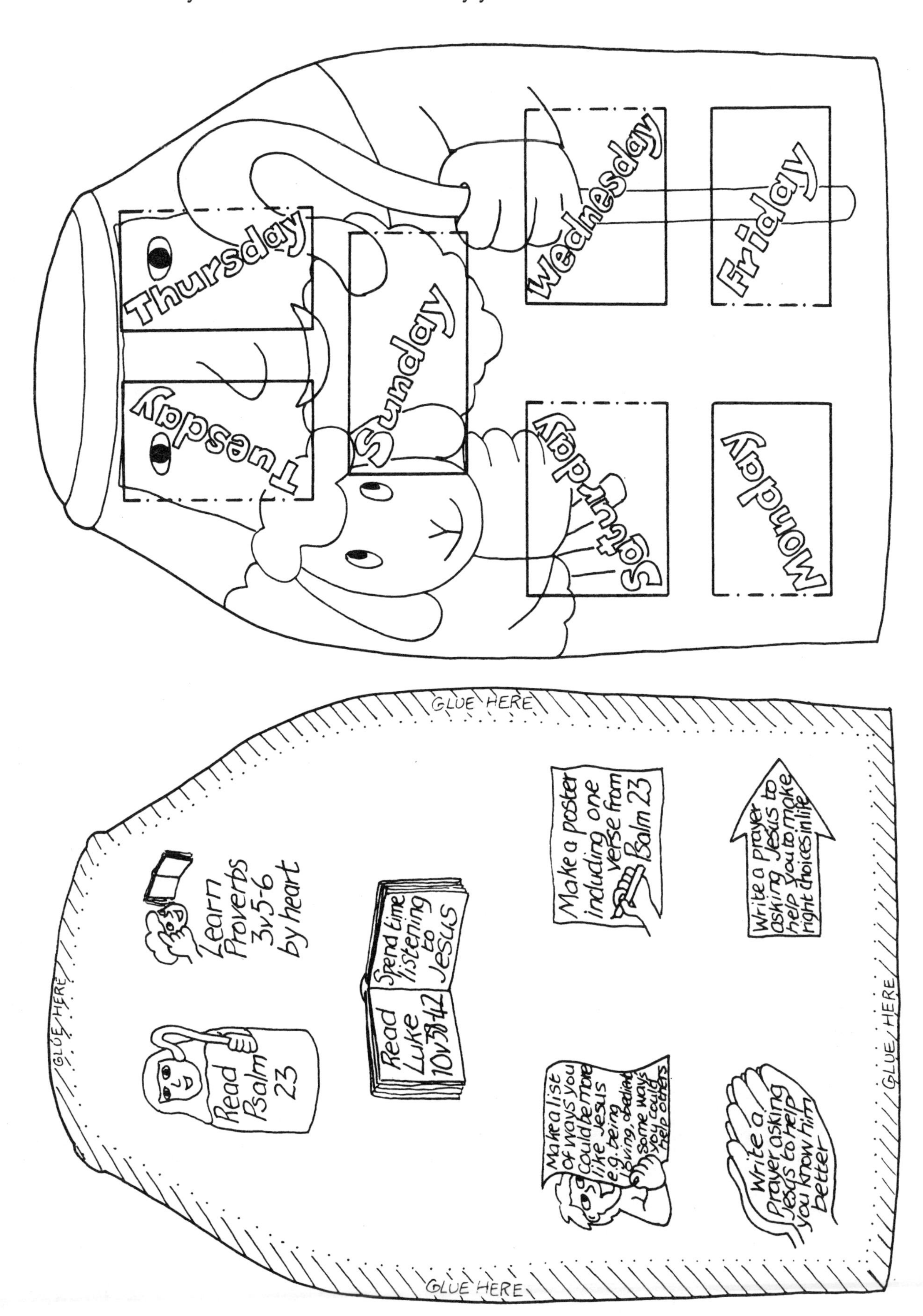

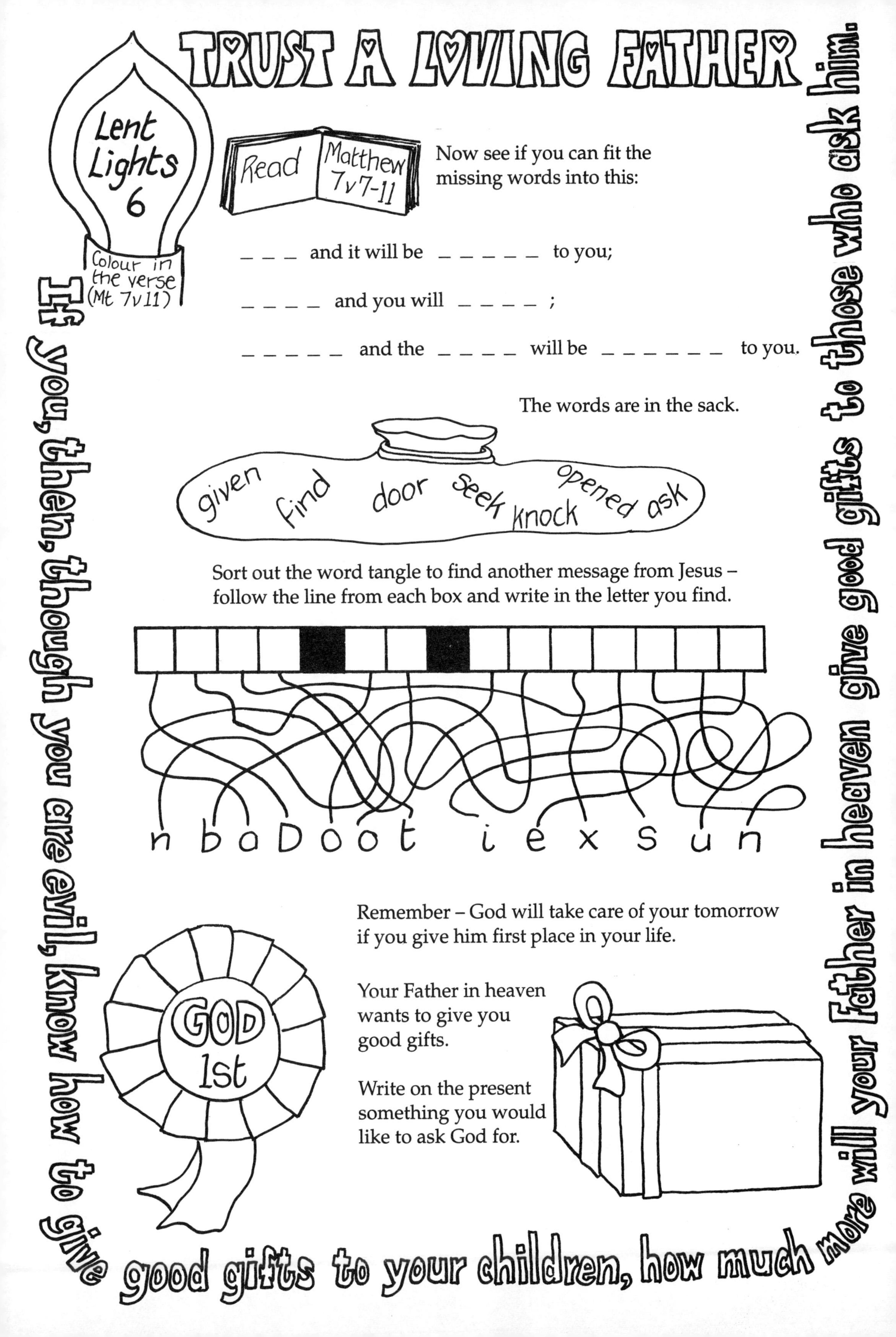
TRUST A LOVING FATHER
Lent Lights 6
Colour in the verse (Mt 7v11)
Read Matthew 7v7-11
Now see if you can fit the missing words into this:
___ and it will be _____ to you;
____ and you will ____ ;
_____ and the ____ will be _______ to you.
The words are in the sack.
given find door seek knock opened ask
Sort out the word tangle to find another message from Jesus – follow the line from each box and write in the letter you find.
n b a D o o t i e x S u n
Remember – God will take care of your tomorrow if you give him first place in your life.
GOD 1st
Your Father in heaven wants to give you good gifts.
Write on the present something you would like to ask God for.
If you, then, though you are evil, know how to give good gifts to your children, how much more will your Father in heaven give good gifts to those who ask him.

18. LENT LIGHTS 6 – TRUST A LOVING FATHER – GOD'S GIFT BOX

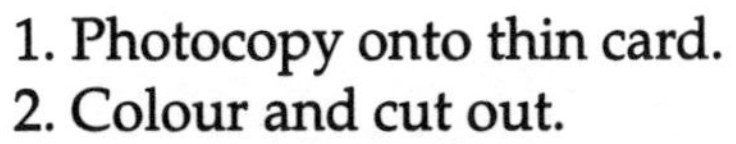

1. Photocopy onto thin card.
2. Colour and cut out.
3. Fold all foldlines outwards.
4. Glue tabs and make up box.
5. Write your name on the gift tag.
6. Write on the doves some gifts God has given you – they may be good things, or they may be gifts God has given you to be good at and use. Some examples:-
   singing, helping, drawing, loving others, dancing, being happy and cheerful, good at sports, drawing, giving . . . and there are lots more.

19. EASTER MOBILE – PART ONE

1. Photocopy this **and** following three pages (20, 21, 22) onto thin card.
2. Colour and cut out – be careful not to cut off 'hangers'.
3. Glue matching pieces back to back – for strength and design on both sides.
4. Assemble your mobile while holding top piece – find the balance point with all pieces on, then hang mobile from here.

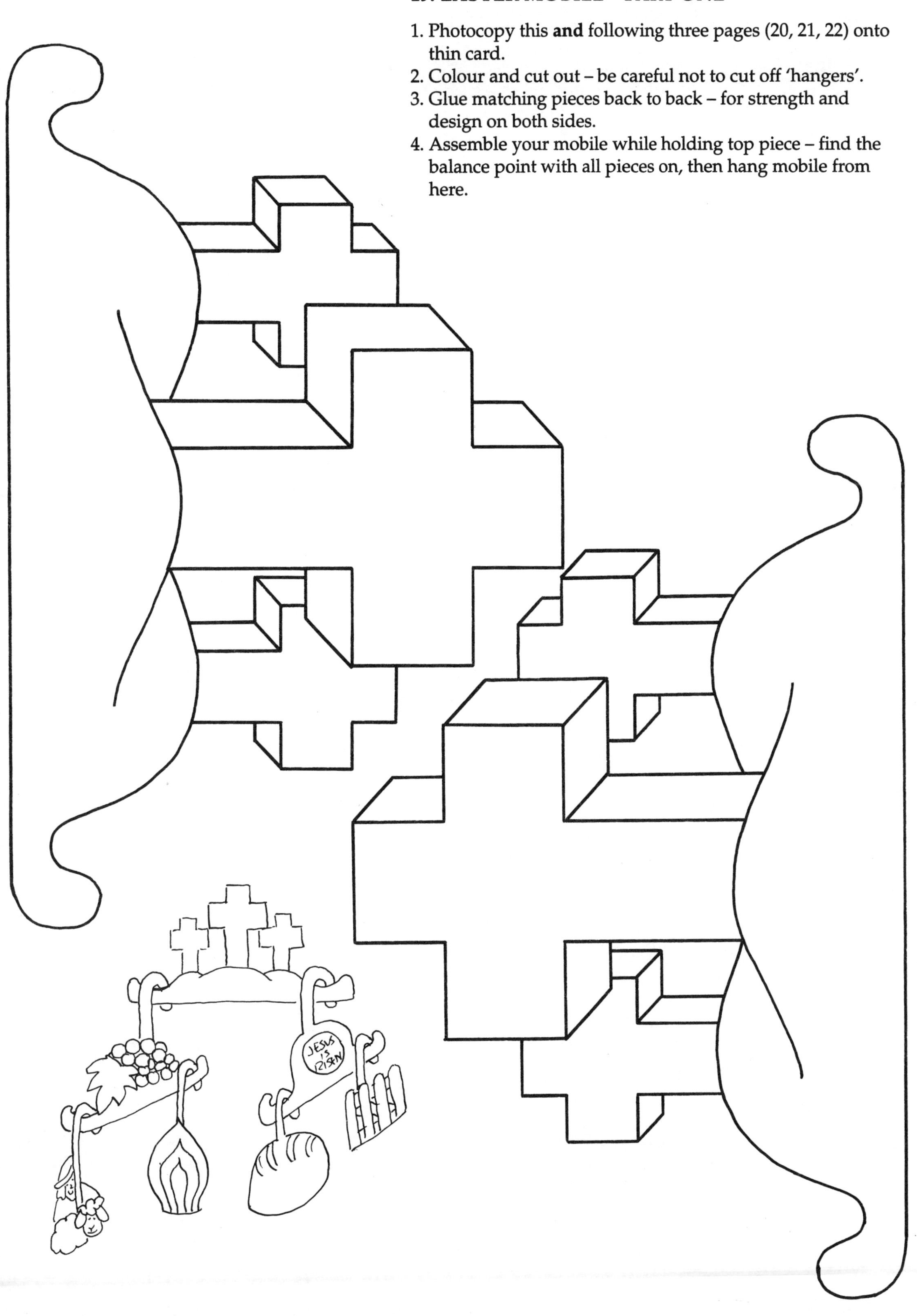

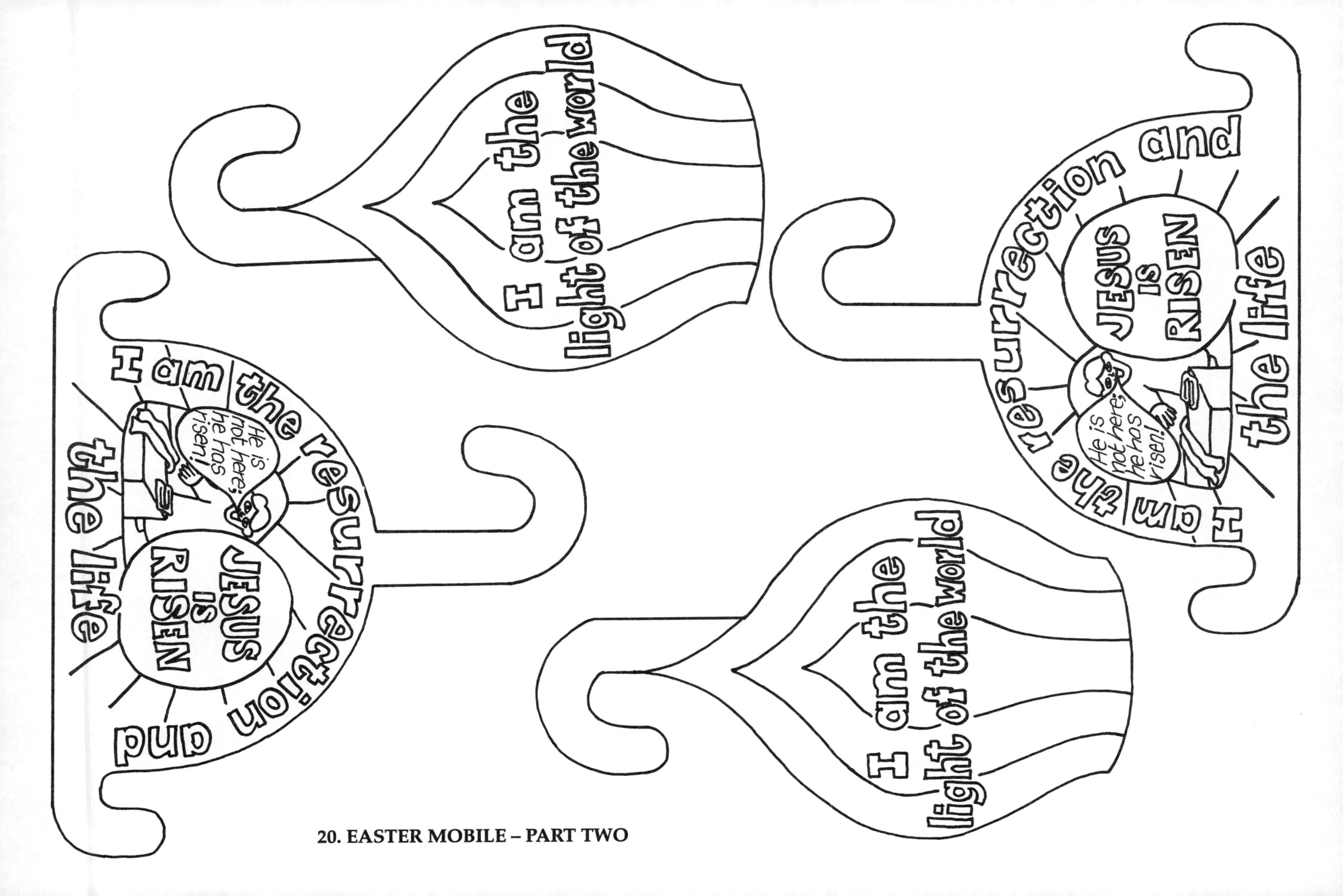

20. EASTER MOBILE – PART TWO

21. EASTER MOBILE – PART THREE

I am
the good
Shepherd
I am
the good
Shepherd

I am the gate
for the sheep
I am the gate
for the sheep

23. EASTER 3-D MODEL – FIGURES 1

1. Photocopy this **and** following four pages onto thin card.
2. Cut out and colour in.
3. Fold all figures on foldlines – glue figures together at top tab. Figures can be moved around model.

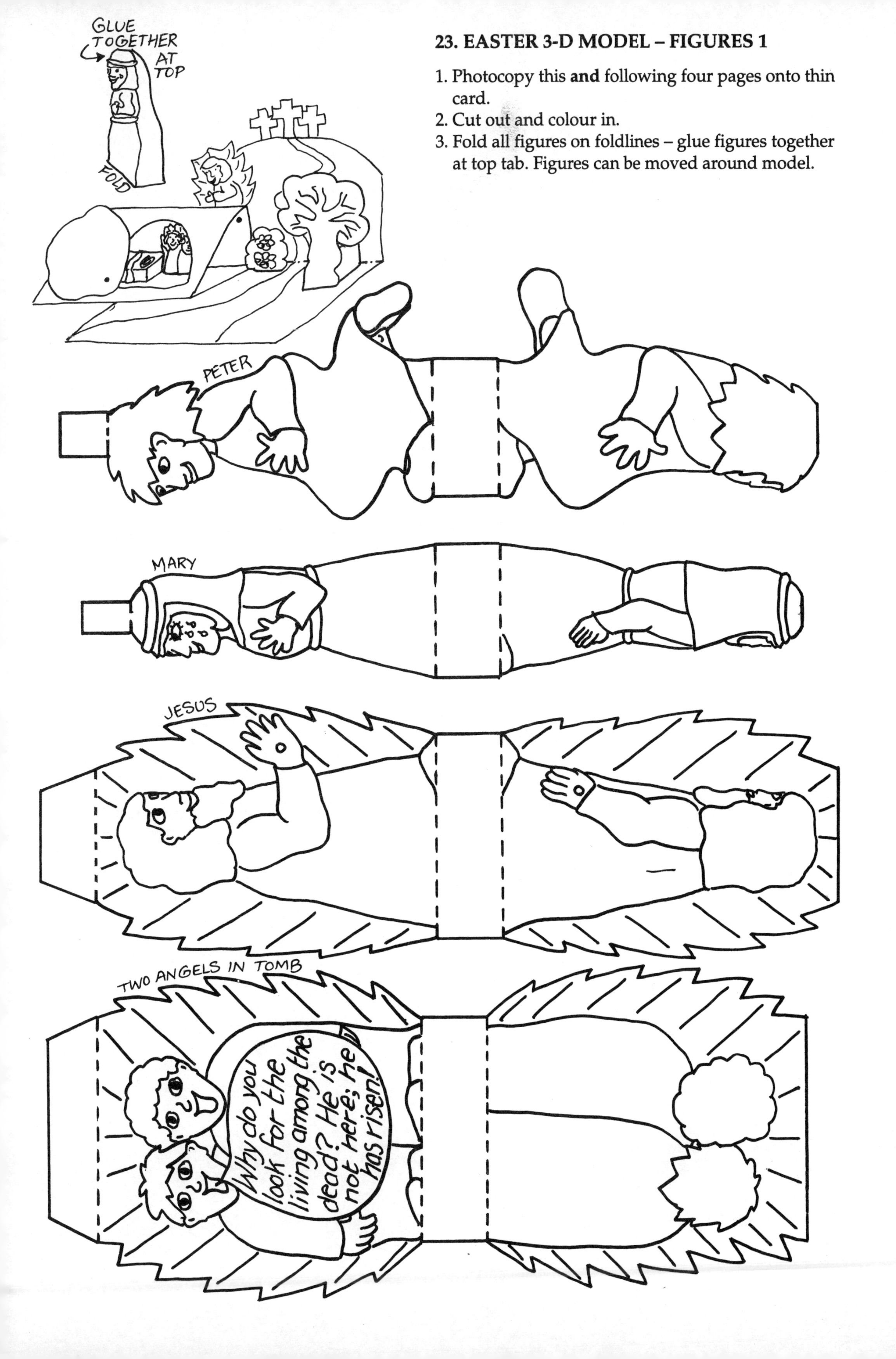

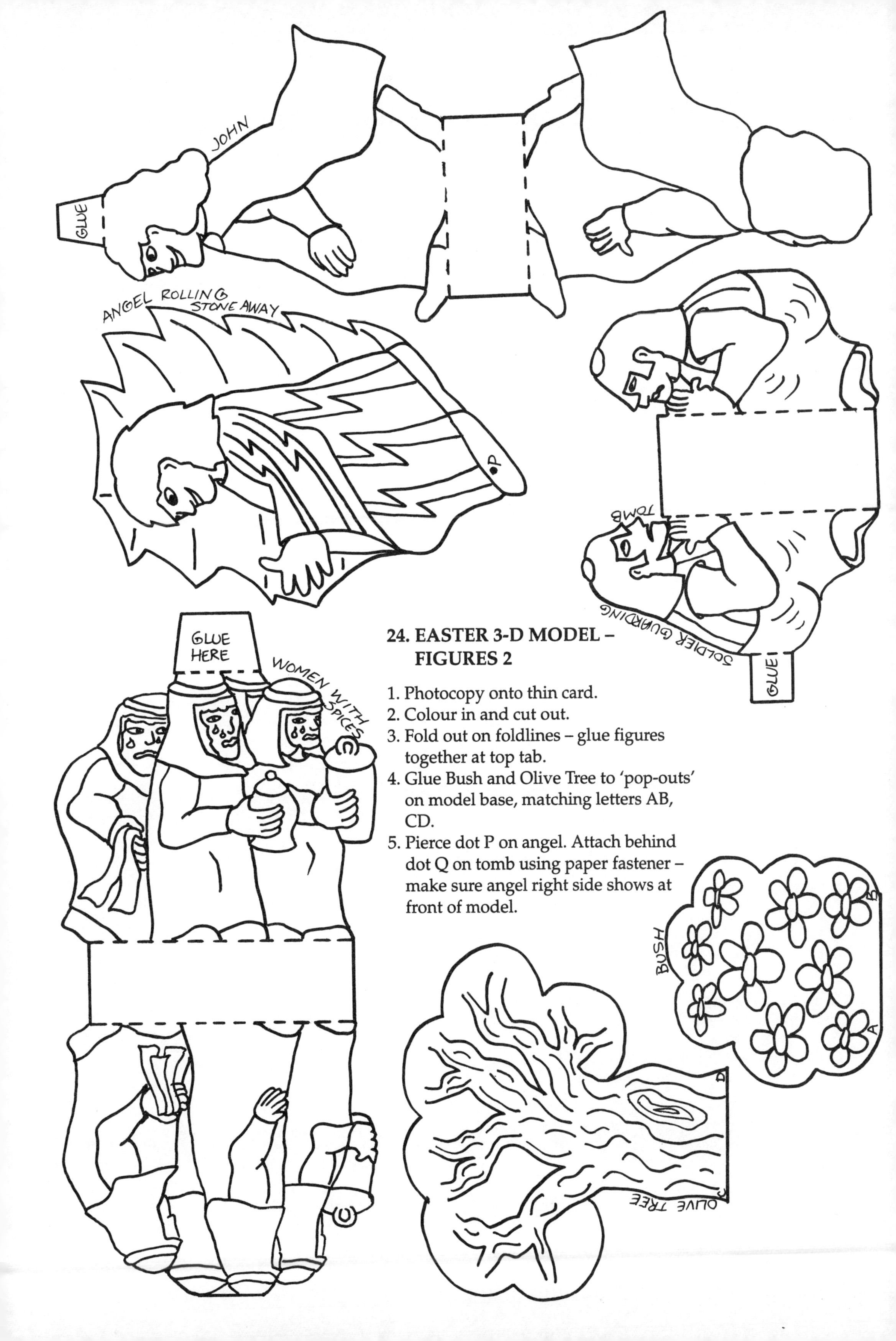

24. EASTER 3-D MODEL – FIGURES 2

1. Photocopy onto thin card.
2. Colour in and cut out.
3. Fold out on foldlines – glue figures together at top tab.
4. Glue Bush and Olive Tree to 'pop-outs' on model base, matching letters AB, CD.
5. Pierce dot P on angel. Attach behind dot Q on tomb using paper fastener – make sure angel right side shows at front of model.

25. EASTER 3-D MODEL – TOMB

1. Photocopy onto thin card.
2. Colour and cut out.
3. Pierce dots X and Q.
4. Cut out large window.
5. Glue into triangular shape with long tab JK.
6. Attach angel with paper fastener through Q then P.
7. Attach stone with paper fastener through Y then X.
8. Glue end of tomb to base, lining up EF and GH.

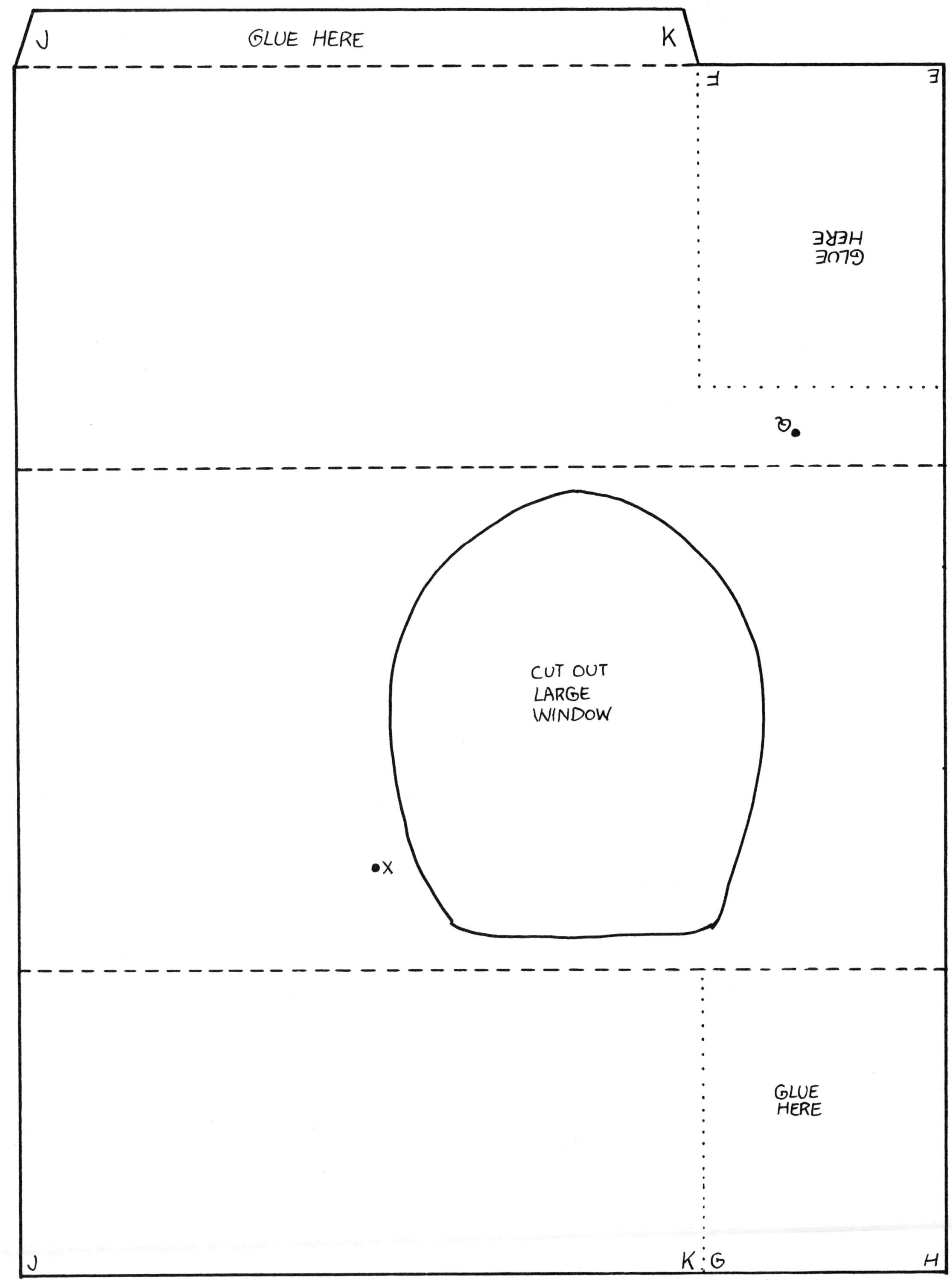

26. EASTER 3-D MODEL – BASE

1. Photocopy onto thin card.
2. Cut slits SA, TB, LC, MD.
4. Fold all foldlines - - - outwards
   - · - · - · inwards.

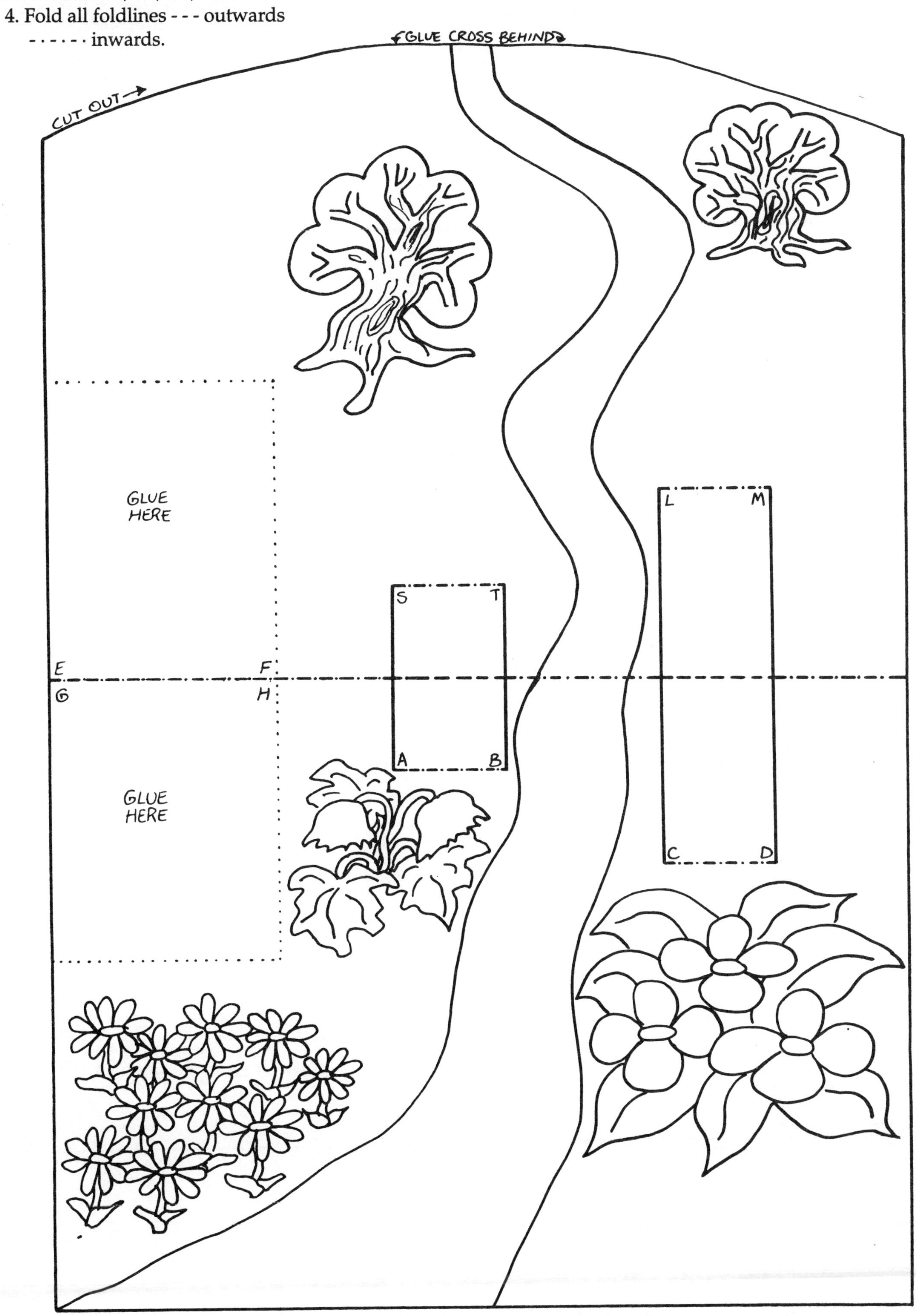

27. EASTER 3-D MODEL – STONE, SHELF, BURIAL CLOTH, CROSS

1. Photocopy onto thin card.
2. Colour and cut out.
3. Fold all foldlines - - - outwards.
4. Glue tabs on tomb shelf and make into box shape.
5. Lay linen strips over this tomb shelf; fold head cloth and put on shelf.
6. Glue cross at top of hill on base.

STONE - ATTACH TO TOMB WITH PAPER FASTENER THROUGH Y THEN X.

Y

FOLD UP HEAD CLOTH

CROSS

DO NOT FOLD

GLUE HERE

TOMB SHELF

GLUE HERE

LINEN STRIPS

MAKE TOMB SHELF

LAY LINEN STRIPS OVER AND PUT FOLDED HEAD CLOTH AT ONE END - PUT INSIDE TOMB

GLUE HERE

GLUE HERE

28. EASTER FRIEZE – PART ONE

1. You will need this **and** following 4 pages (29-32) – or they can be used as individual colouring sheets.
2. Photocopy onto paper or thin card.
3. Cut along top outline and along two of the straight edges – leave right hand edge on, to glue next picture to this.

29. EASTER FRIEZE – PART TWO

30. EASTER FRIEZE – PART THREE

CUT ALONG OUTLINE

Friday

31. EASTER FRIEZE – PART FOUR

32. EASTER FRIEZE – PART FIVE

33. OPEN DOOR EASTER CARD – PART ONE

1. Photocopy this page onto paper **and** following page onto thin card.
2. Cut out and colour.
3. Cut round slit XY on stone door of tomb – but **do not** cut dotted line.
4. Fold outwards on central dotted line - - - and inwards on edge of stone - · - · - · -
5. Glue 'Jesus is risen' on inside of card in a position so that you can read 'Jesus is risen' when stone door is opened.

Happy
Easter
Love from

35. EASTER POP-UP – PART ONE

1. Photocopy this **and** following page onto thin card.
2. Colour and cut out.
3. Fold all foldlines - - - - outwards - · - · - · - inwards
4. Glue tabs A, B, C, D, E, F to marked positions on base.
5. Fold card then open to see 'pop-up'.

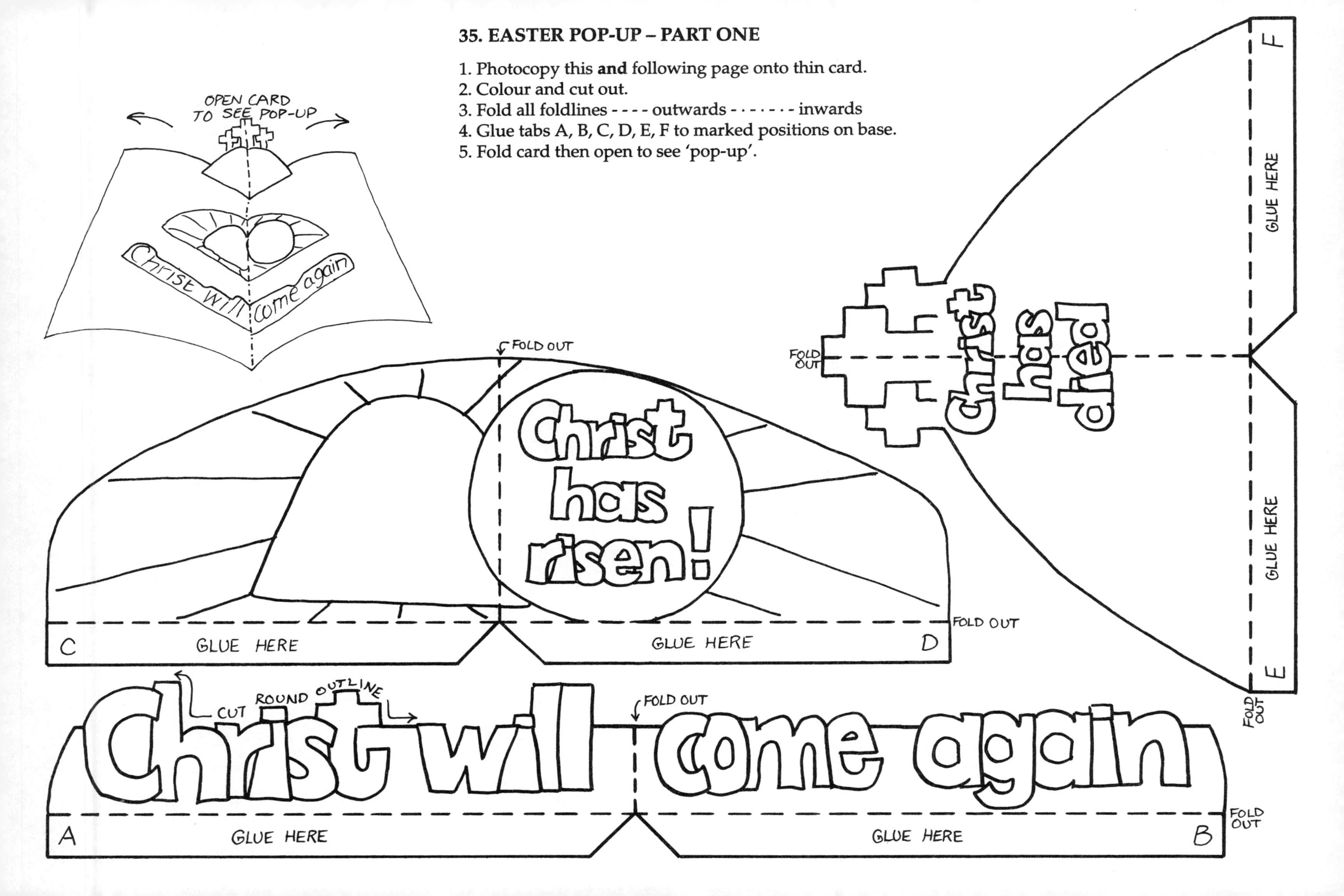

36. EASTER POP-UP – PART TWO – BASE

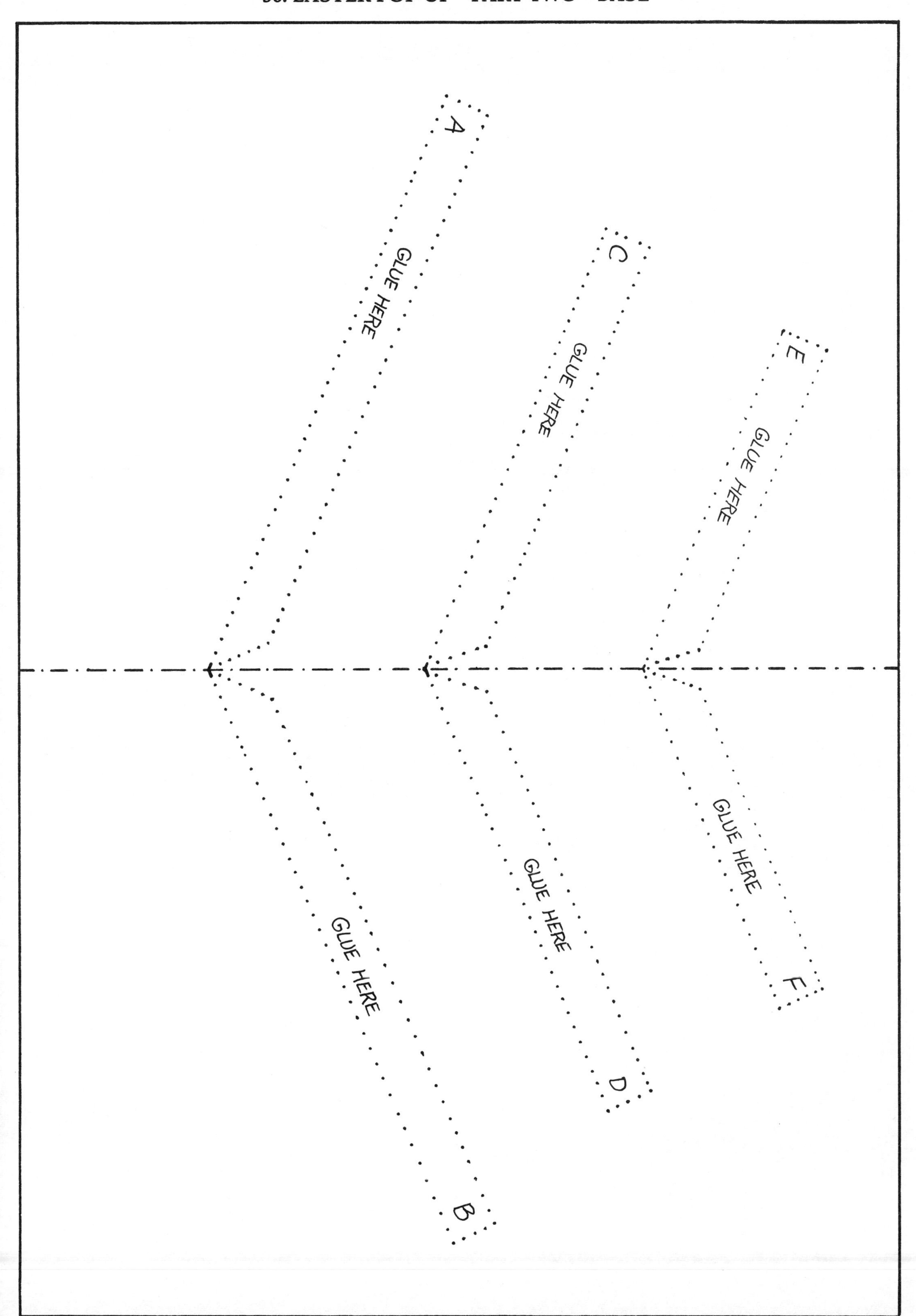

37. PROPHECIES ABOUT JESUS' DEATH – SPINNER PART ONE

1. Photocopy this **and** following page onto thin card.
2. Colour and cut out.
3. Cut out two windows in top circle (this page).
4. Pierce holes A and B, then join two circles with paper fastener through A then B.
5. Turn top circle to read off prophecies and fulfilments about Jesus' birth. Look up the bible references for more detail. See from the timeline how long before Jesus the prophets lived.

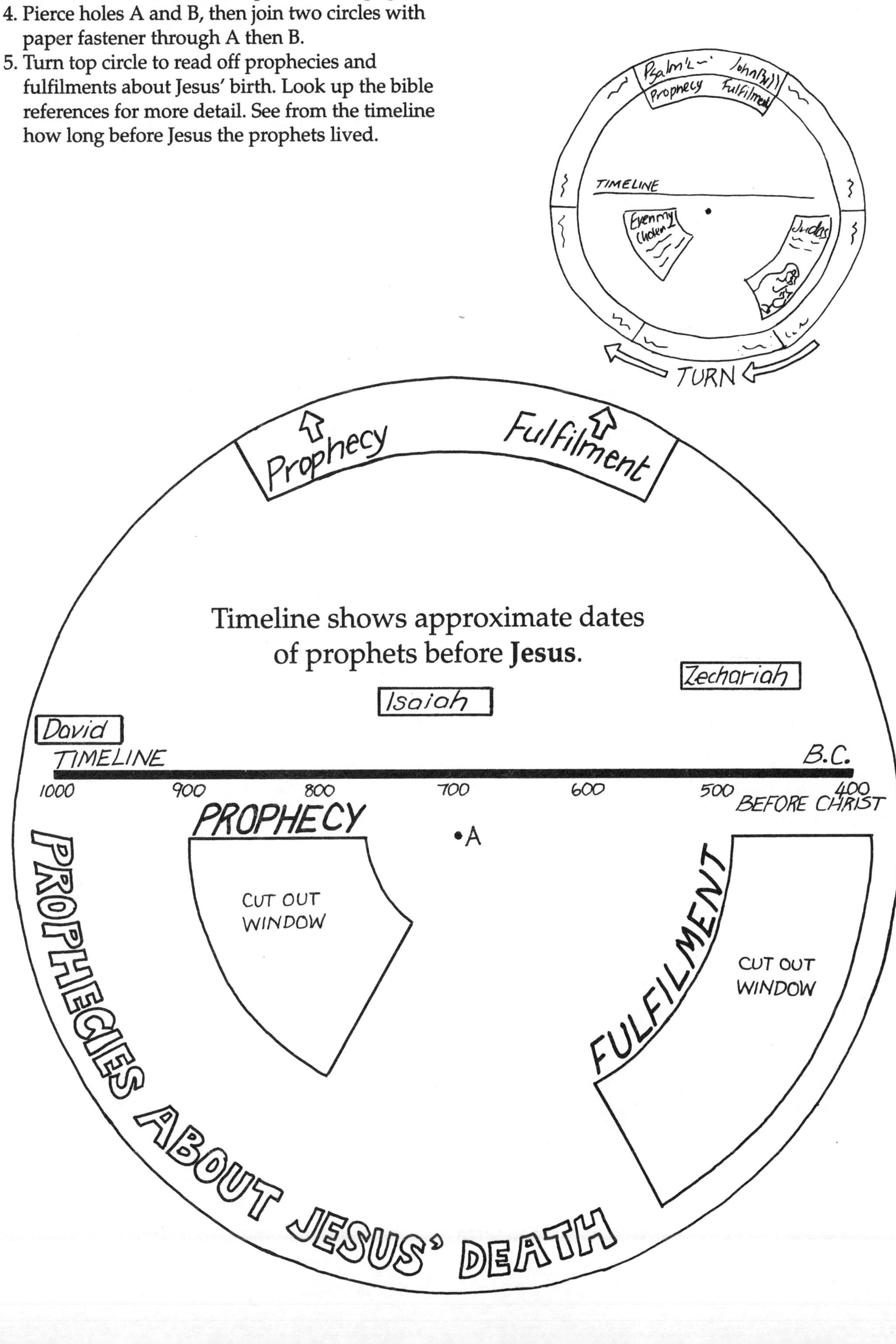

38. PROPHECIES ABOUT JESUS' DEATH – SPINNER PART TWO

See previous page for instructions.

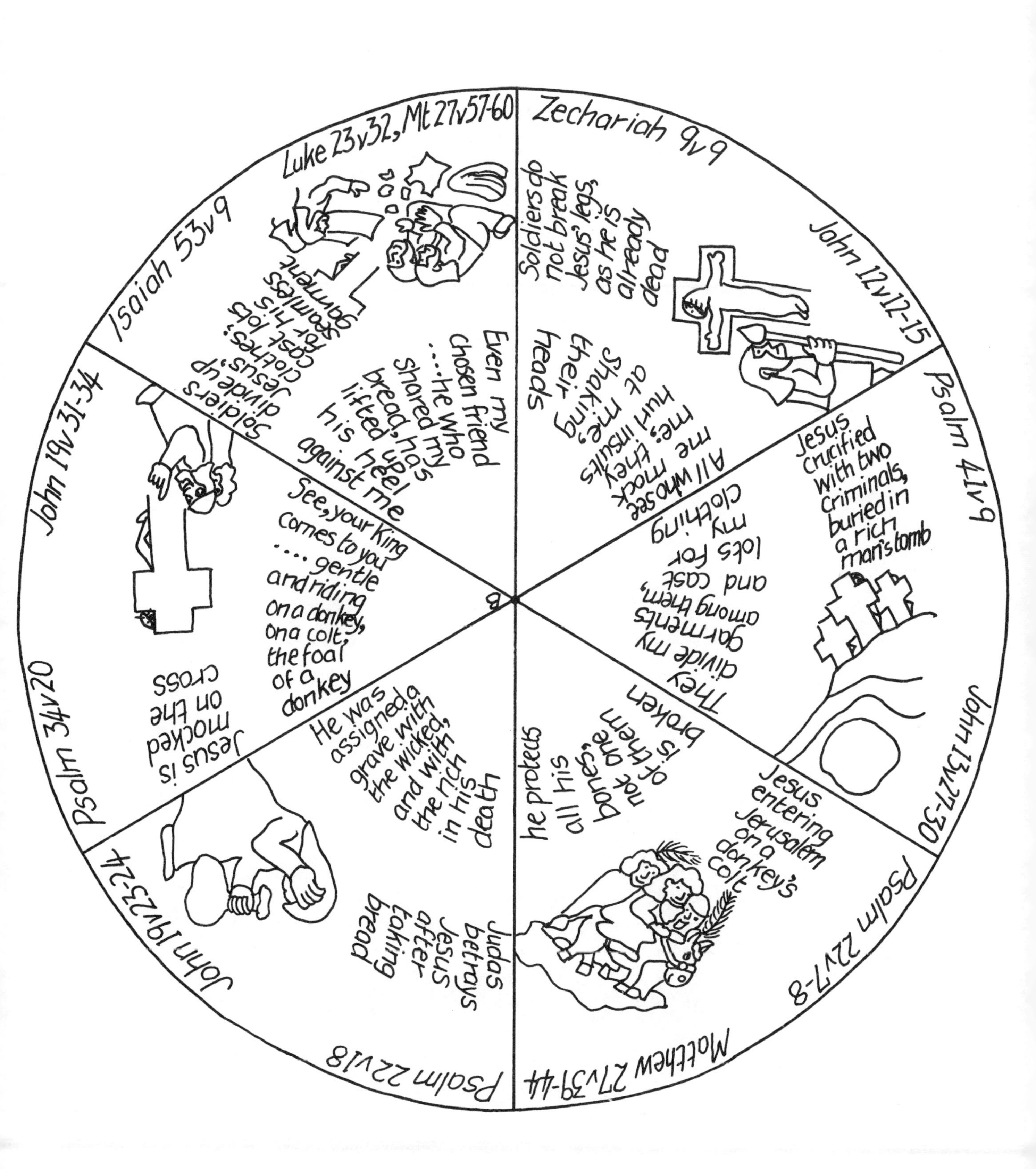

39. JESUS ENTERS JERUSALEM – DONKEY MODEL

1. Photocopy onto thin card.
2. Colour and cut out all pieces.
3. Fold outwards on foldlines.
4. Cut slit AB.
5. Glue donkey head onto marked position on body.
6. Glue donkey ears onto head, one each side.
7. Slot figure into slit AB to see Jesus ride the donkey's colt.

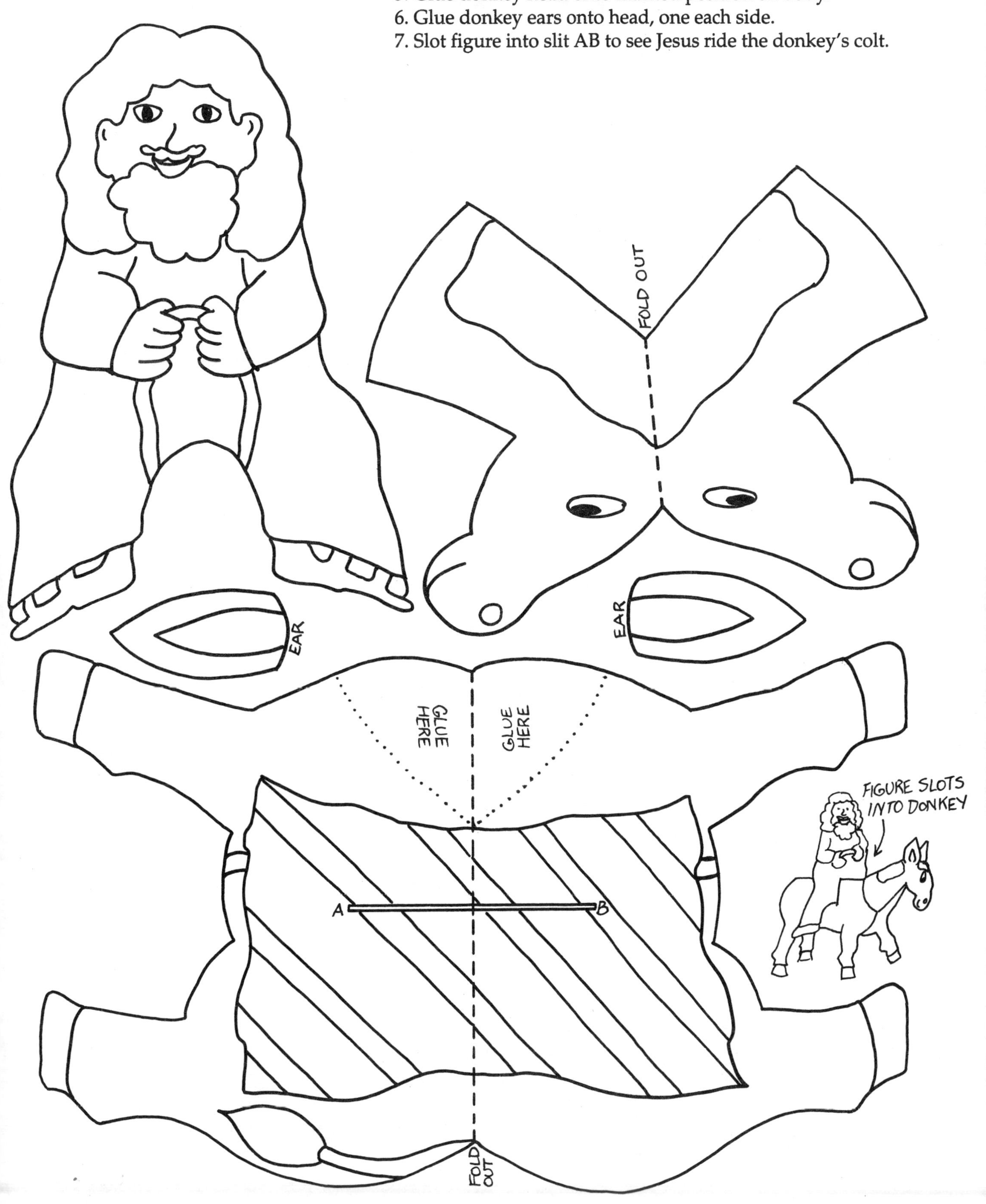

40. LAST SUPPER – SCENE WITH SPEECH BUBBLES

1. Photocopy onto thin card.
2. Colour and cut out.
3. Pierce dots A, B – attach wheel behind model with paper fastener through A then B.
4. Glue small tabs and fix speech bubbles above heads of correct disciples (see John 13-14).
5. Cut strip of card 2.5 cm by 29 cm. Fold over 2 cm tab at each end – glue to back of model to stand up.
6. Turn wheel to read Jesus' answers to disciples.

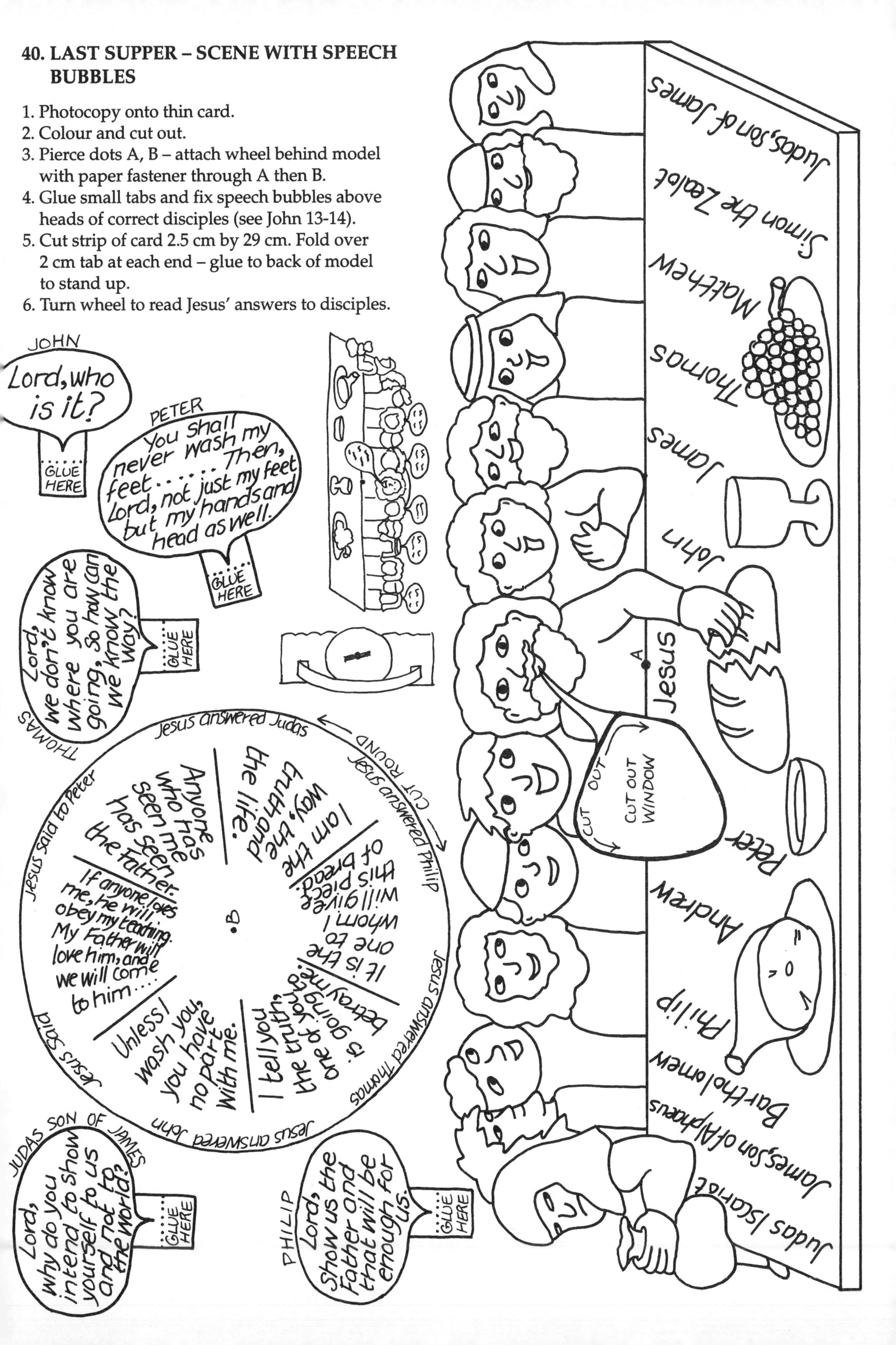

41. JESUS' ARREST – DRESSING FIGURE PART ONE – LUKE 22:54-23:25

1. Photocopy this page onto thin card and following page onto paper.
2. Colour and cut out – glue front to back of dressing figure.
3. Fold outwards on foldlines of both stands – glue tabs and glue to back of Jesus and dressing figure. Glue stands 0.5 cm from bottom of figures so they lean back very slightly.

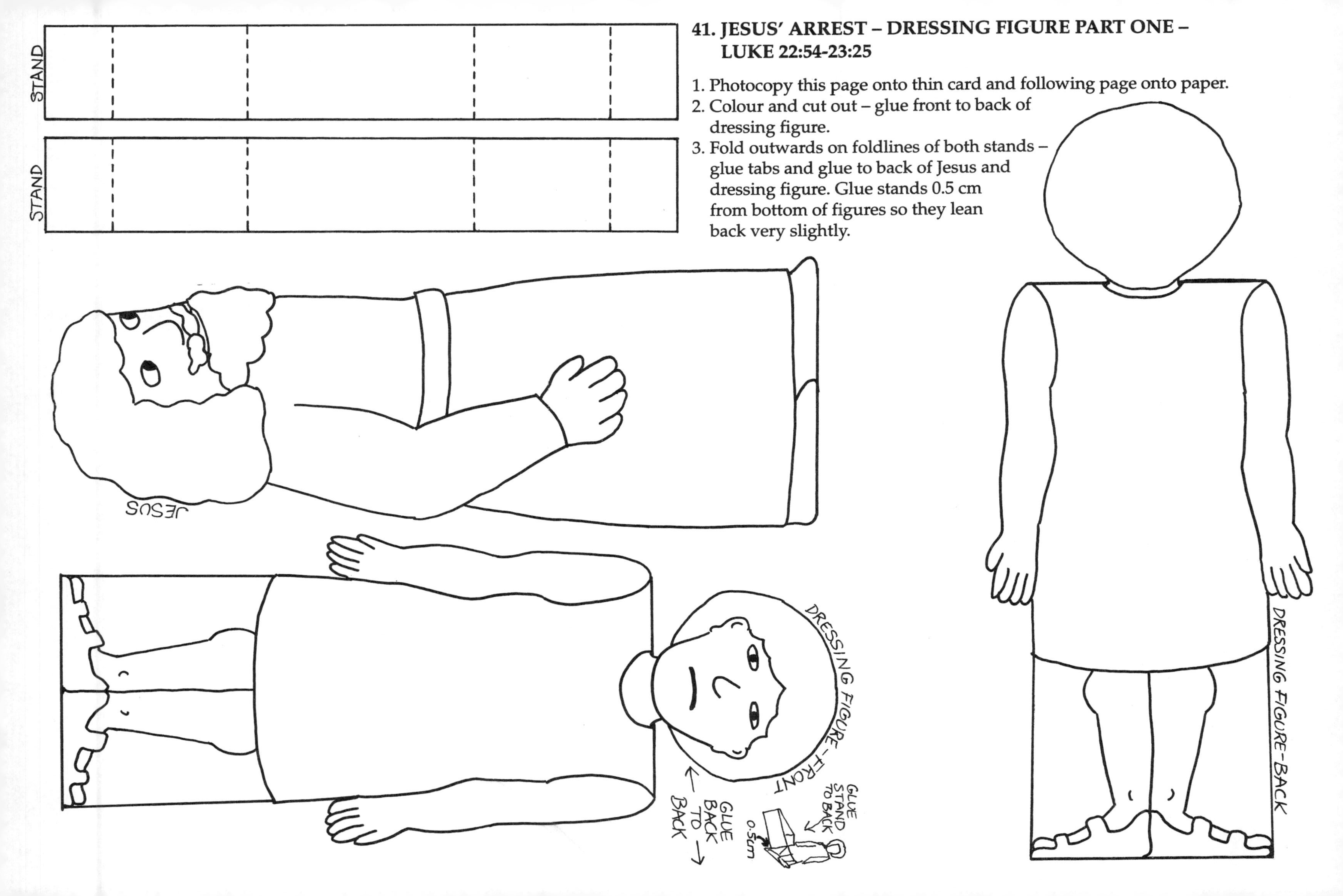

42. JESUS' ARREST – DRESSING FIGURE PART TWO – CLOTHES

1. Photocopy onto paper.
2. Colour and cut out.
3. Fold back tabs along dotted lines - - - -.
4. Dress the figure in different clothes to make Jesus appear before different characters, or be arrested by a soldier (see Luke 22:54-23:25).

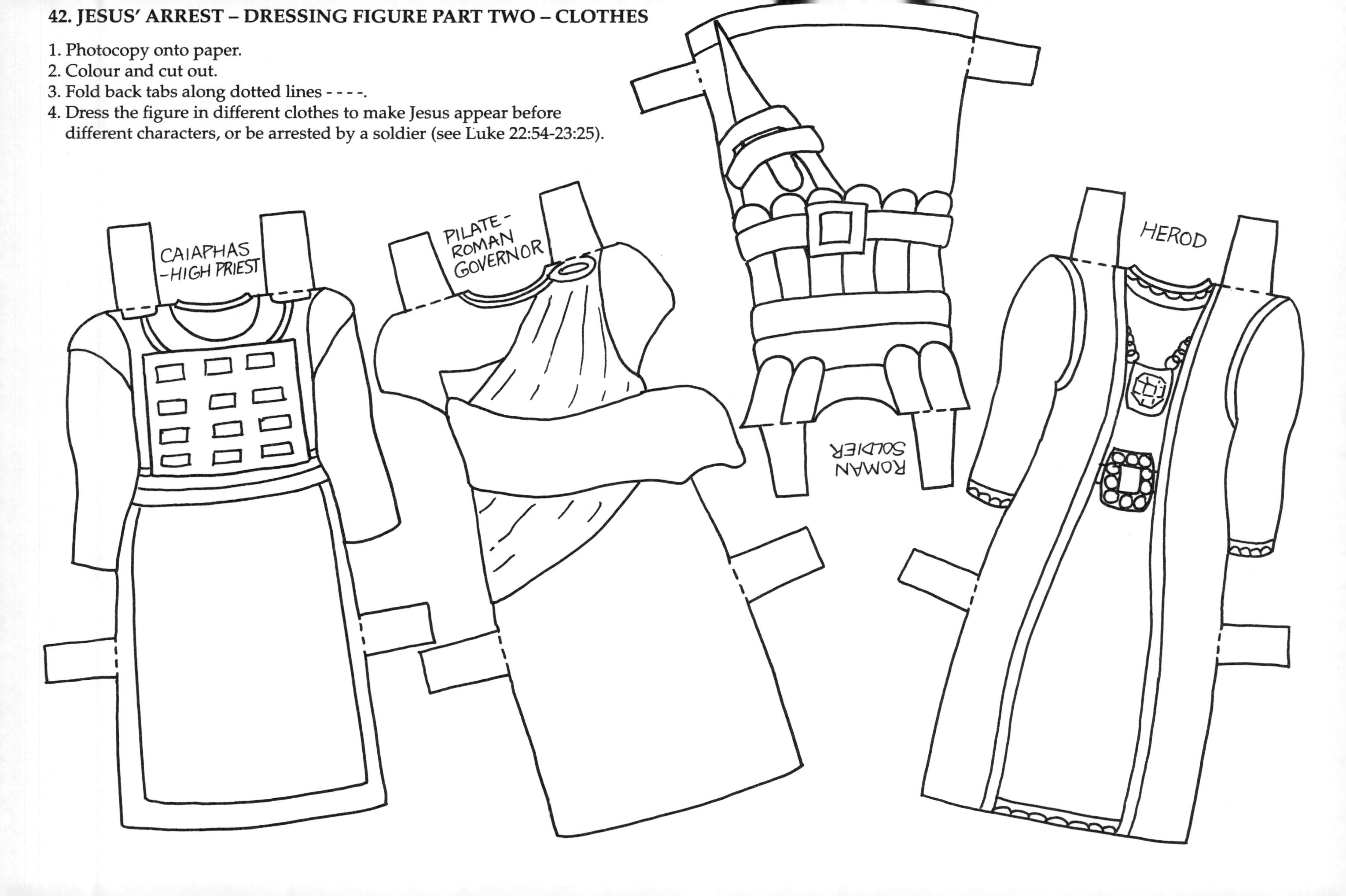

43. JESUS' LAST WEEK – JERUSALEM MAP PUZZLE

1. Photocopy onto paper.
2. Cut out the 8 small squares.
3. Look up the Bible reference to see what happened there.
4. Glue small squares in position on map according to their map reference.

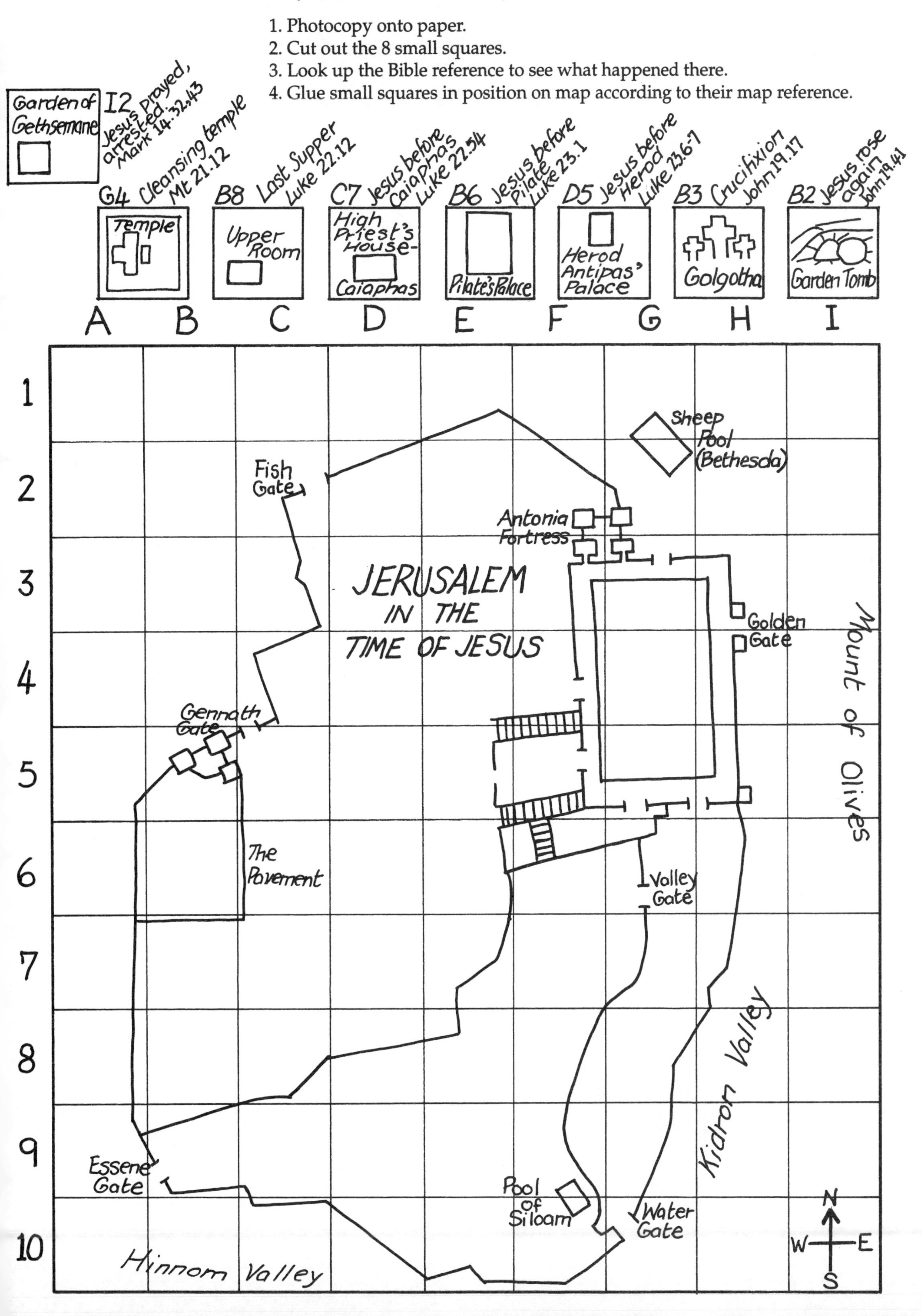

44. JESUS' RESURRECTION APPEARANCES – FIND THE ORDER PUZZLE

1. Photocopy onto thin card.
2. Colour and cut out the 8 cards.
3. See if you can put them in the order in which they happened – as a clue there is a number hidden in each picture.
4. You can make a 'mini frieze' by gluing them onto a long narrow strip of card or stiff paper.

45. EASTER WINDOW PICTURE

1. Photocopy onto **tracing paper** – use good quality tracing paper, obtainable from art/stationers' shops in A4 size – this should be hand fed through the photocopier.
2. Colour using felt-tip pens for translucent effect.
3. Stick to a window using sticky putty.

46. EASTER CROSSWORD

Across

1. The high priest (8)
3. Missing for Jesus' first resurrection appearance to the disciples in the upper room (6)
7. Pieces of silver Judas received (6)
8. These items of linen were lying in the empty tomb (6)
11. The Roman governor (6)
12. Means 'place of the skull' (8)
14. Peter denied Jesus this many times (5)
15. Carried Jesus into Jerusalem (6)
17. It was like drops of blood as Jesus prayed earnestly in Gethsemane (5)
18. He betrayed Jesus (5)
19. Name of the feast day when the last supper took place (8)
20. Jesus broke this at the last supper (5)
22. Released instead of Jesus (8)
24. Last supper eaten here (5, 4)

Down

2. Home of man who placed Jesus's body in his own tomb (9)
4. Chief priests felt this for Jesus (4)
5. Girl who was this in the high priest's house asked Peter if he knew Jesus (4)
6. Who rolled away the stone of the tomb (5)
9. Jesus rose again on this day (6)
10. Taken with perfumes by the women to anoint Jesus' body (6)
12. Jesus arrested here (10)
13. Number of criminals crucified with Jesus (3)
16. Judas did this to Jesus to betray him (6)
19. Disciple who cut off the high priest's servant's ear at Jesus' arrest (5)
21. The sky was this as Jesus died (4)

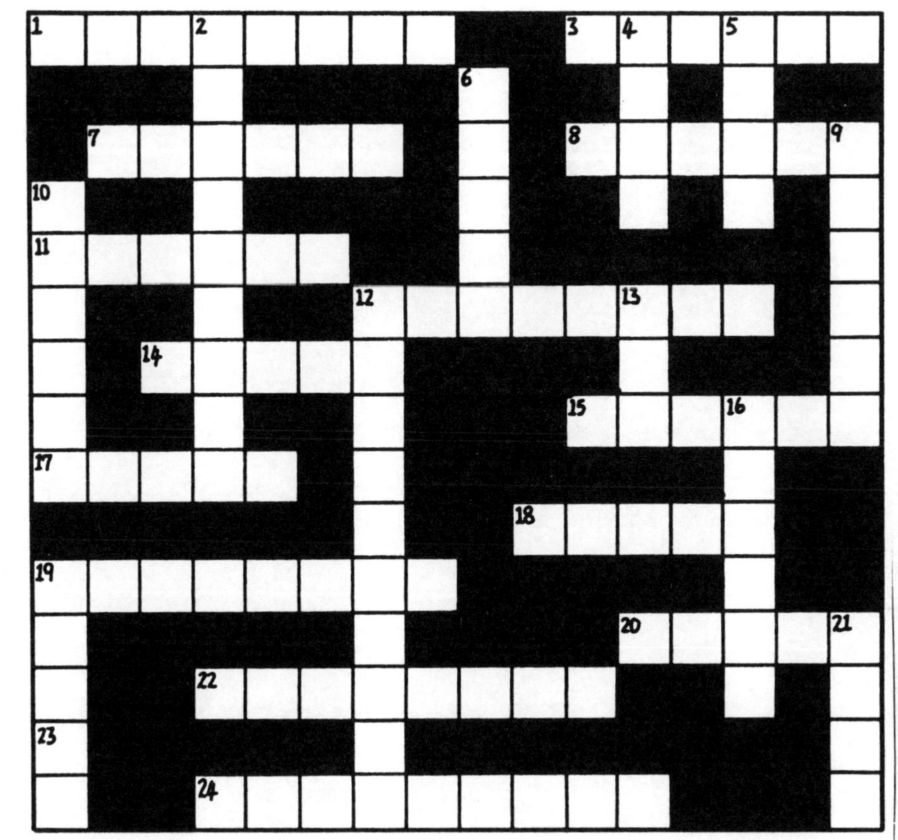

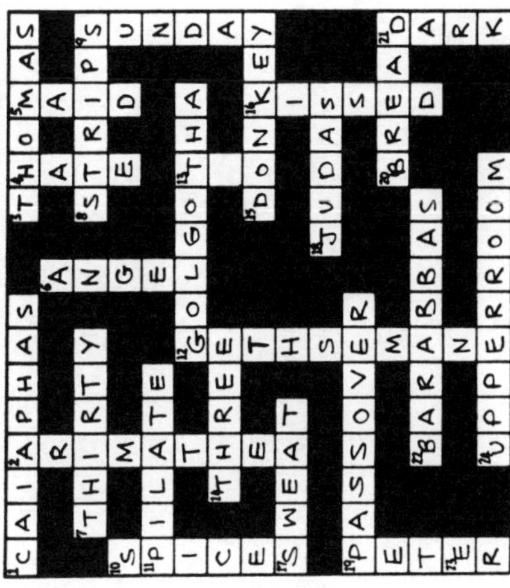

Solution to crossword
(this can be covered when you
are making photocopies)